**Selling like a hero: awaken your courage
and overcome sales challenges**

Copyright © 2024 Reginaldo Osnildo

I0422608

REGINALDO OSNILDO

PRESENTATION

It is with great enthusiasm that I share my passion for archetypes, more precisely the use of archetypes in sales narratives. This book, in particular, which will emphasize the hero archetype, entitled **Selling like a hero: awaken your courage and overcome sales challenges**, has been carefully developed to provide you with practical, actionable knowledge that will boost your sales and results.

As the author of this book, I have dedicated my career to the mission of humanizing companies and helping them create an authentic and meaningful presence in the marketplace. My background as a doctoral professor at the University of Southern Santa Catarina, combined with my experience as a strategist at the SCONTIME Agency and the Catarinense Radio Group, has given me the opportunity to explore the potential of narratives, archetypes and magical tools such as artificial intelligence.

I deeply believe in the transformative power of narratives and their ability to engage and enchant the target audience. As a researcher, I focused my doctorate in Language Sciences on the study of sales narratives using mental triggers and digital convergence, while my master's degree explored the connection between storytelling and the social imaginary. In addition, I began my academic journey by studying for a bachelor's degree in Social Communication, with a major in Journalism, also at the University of Southern Santa Catarina.

A journalist by training, I believe that the true power of a book lies in its ability to become a tool for transformation. Get ready to unlock your full potential and achieve extraordinary results. Whenever necessary, I will refer to works from a wide range of fields.

In the book *The Hero and the Outlaw: How to Build Extraordinary Brands Using the Power of Archetypes*, for example, authors Margaret Mark and Carol Pearson are spot on in establishing a map for managing the meaning of brands. When I read this work for my doctoral thesis, I learned many things, one of which came from the following sentence: "In increasingly spiritual times, the courage and perseverance of the hero can be promoted as necessary factors for spiritual fulfillment."

I wondered if this spirituality could be human potency itself and, thus, could the archetype directed towards activation shape new heroes? I'll go further. My thesis looked at archetypes in sales. Could the hero archetype be activated in salespeople and make them sell like heroes? You may be wondering now if the answer is here in this book. Maybe that's why you bought it. After all, the title makes that provocation. But I'd like to make it clear that the answer lies with you. It is you, the seller, who will activate the hero. My role with this book will be to show you the map for this journey.

It will be in the day-to-day world of sales that a shining path will reveal itself to those who dare to walk it with bravery and determination. This path, which I'm going to call "The path of the sales hero", is an exciting journey that invites every salesperson to become a protagonist in their quest for success. I hope you'll be with me to the end and that you'll be able to tell me if you've made it.

Count on me on this journey of discovery and growth. Let's turn your vision into reality and achieve the success you deserve!

With enthusiasm,

Your mentor on this journey,

Prof. Dr. Reginaldo Osnildo.

CHAPTER 1: THE PATH AND ATTRIBUTES OF THE SALES HERO

In the depths of the sales world, a shining path reveals itself to those who dare to walk it with bravery and determination. This path is an exciting journey that invites every salesperson to become a true protagonist in their quest for success.

Just as in the epic tales that have inspired generations, the hero's journey in sales is full of challenges and obstacles that test salespeople's courage, resilience and ability to overcome. Every salesperson who embarks on this journey must face their own internal dragons - the fear of failure, uncertainty in the face of adversity and the doubts that try to undermine their confidence.

However, the true sales hero finds strength in their purpose and their passion for offering solutions that transform customers' lives. They understand that their mission goes beyond mere business transactions; it's about creating authentic connections, fulfilling needs and bringing smiles of satisfaction to every customer they serve.

But the path of the sales hero is not only about an altruistic quest for the good of customers, but also a quest for self-discovery and constant improvement. The sales hero must master their communication skills, the art of persuasion and in-depth knowledge of their product or service. They must be prepared to adapt to market changes and learn from their experiences, seeking growth and improvement in every interaction.

Wisdom is an indispensable ally for the sales hero. They understand that, just like the trajectory of great leaders and mentors, their journey is marked by learning and teaching. The sales hero is open to knowledge, seeks out valuable insights and shares their experiences with teammates so that everyone can prosper together.

Along the sales hero's path, resilience reveals itself as an essential virtue. Falls and obstacles are part of the journey, but the true hero rises with renewed strength after each setback. He knows that it is in the difficulties that the greatest lessons are learned, and it is with this conviction that he persists in his mission.

Enthusiasm and passion are the flame that drives the sales hero to go beyond his own limits. He infects his clients and colleagues with positive energy, making every interaction not just a transaction, but a memorable and enriching experience for both parties.

The hero's path in sales is a journey of self-discovery, transformation and continuous growth. It reminds us that, despite the challenges, every salesperson has within them the potential to be a sales hero and, with bravery, can achieve extraordinary results.

As you embark on this journey, this book becomes a valuable compass, guiding you, the salesperson, towards the pinnacle of your skills, providing insights and strategies that will help you stand out in your career. Remember, you are the protagonist of this narrative and sales success awaits you at the end of the hero's journey.

Don't think that we're talking here about superheroes from movies or comic books. There is a whole narrative and anthropological theory behind hero narratives. Mythologist Joseph Campbell wrote the book The Hero with a Thousand Faces, which deals with everyday heroes. In the context of his research, everyday heroes were present in mythical narratives spread across all continents. He identified a common pattern in these narratives, only the faces changed. The goal was the same: to accept the challenge, face it and come back victorious.

At the heart of every great salesperson lies a potential hero as strong as those who brought ancient myths to life, whose extraordinary attributes and skills are the key to winning the hearts and minds of customers. Just like the protagonists of the legends, the sales hero is endowed with remarkable qualities that set him apart and enable him to face challenges with fearlessness and achieve exceptional results.

Unshakeable courage:

The first and most remarkable attribute of the sales hero is his unwavering courage. He faces each sales day as an adventure, without fear of the unknown or possible difficulties. The sales hero's courage drives him to approach potential clients with confidence, overcome objections with determination and face obstacles with bravery. He understands that courage is the driving force that guides him towards success, allowing him to go beyond the limits of the ordinary and turn every challenge into an opportunity for growth.

Empathy and compassion:

The sales hero is a true master in the art of empathy and compassion. They genuinely put themselves in the customer's shoes, seeking to understand their needs, desires and concerns. This ability to connect emotionally allows the sales hero to build authentic and meaningful relationships, turning every interaction into a human experience, not just a simple business transaction.

Subtle and ethical persuasion:

Unlike the anti-hero, who seeks to manipulate and deceive to achieve his goals, the sales hero uses subtle and ethical persuasion as his secret weapon. They use well-founded arguments, solid evidence and inspiring stories to captivate their customers' minds. The sales hero understands that ethical persuasion is based on mutual trust and transparency, creating lasting bonds with customers.

In-depth and up-to-date knowledge:

The sales hero is a tireless scholar of his trade. He invests time and dedication in deepening his knowledge of the product or service he is offering, as well as the relevant market and trends. This comprehensive and up-to-date knowledge is the basis for offering personalized solutions and precise responses to customer needs, demonstrating authority and credibility in their interactions.

Persistence and resilience:

The path of the sales hero is not without its challenges and adversities. However, their spirit is marked by persistence and resilience. The sales hero learns from failures, gets up after each fall and remains focused on his goals. Their resilience drives them forward even in the face of rejection, turning every obstacle into an opportunity to grow and improve their skills.

Humility and a willingness to learn:

Although endowed with extraordinary skills, the sales hero is humble and recognizes that there is always something new to learn. They are open to feedback, seek out mentors and colleagues to share experiences with and are willing to constantly improve their skills. His incessant search for growth and learning is what makes him an even more powerful sales hero.

The sales hero is not a mythological being or a fanciful creation; he is a real and inspiring figure who resides within every salesperson. Awakening the sales hero in you is an act of self-discovery and self-transformation. By adopting and cultivating these attributes, you, the salesperson, will be prepared to conquer the market, face sales battles with courage and achieve results that go beyond expectations. Be the hero of your own sales story and make your mark as an exceptional salesperson! Venture out, discover your power, conquer the market and be a true sales hero!

The inner courage to face challenges

On our journey as salespeople, we are constantly challenged by situations that test our courage and determination. From the initial approach to a potential client to facing difficult objections, the road to sales is strewn with obstacles that can arouse our fears and insecurities. However, it is in these challenging moments that we have the opportunity to discover and nurture our inner courage, becoming true heroes of our own sales.

Recognizing our fears:

The first step to discovering inner courage is to recognize and accept our fears. We all face moments of doubt and fear, and this is perfectly normal. Identifying our fears allows us to better understand their origin and thus find ways to deal with them effectively. Face your fears head on, because it is through facing them that we begin to build our courage.

Turning fear into a challenge:

Instead of seeing fear as a threat, we should see it as a challenge to be overcome. Courage is not the absence of fear, but the willingness to move forward even in the face of it. Turn your fears into stimulating challenges and see every difficulty as an opportunity to grow and become stronger.

Setting realistic goals:

Setting realistic and achievable goals is fundamental to cultivating inner courage. Divide your challenges into smaller, more manageable stages, setting clear and achievable goals for each phase. As you achieve these small victories, your confidence will grow and your courage will strengthen to face bigger challenges.

Learning from experience:

Every challenge we face in sales is an opportunity to learn and evolve. Regardless of the outcome, view each experience as a valuable lesson. Identify the points where you were successful and the aspects that can be improved. By learning from each experience, you become more resilient and able to deal with future challenges with more confidence.

Seeking support and guidance:

Don't be afraid to seek support and guidance when necessary.

Sharing your experiences with teammates or mentors can provide an outside view that helps you overcome challenges more efficiently. In addition, exchanging knowledge and experiences with other salespeople can be a powerful source of inspiration and encouragement.

Practicing self-care:

Inner courage is also fueled by self-care. Taking care of yourself emotionally, physically and mentally is essential for facing challenges with clarity and resilience. Make time for rest, physical exercise, relaxation practices and leisure time. A salesperson who feels good about themselves will be better able to face the challenges of everyday life.

Visualizing success:

Visualization is a powerful tool for awakening inner courage. Before facing a challenge, take a moment to visualize yourself succeeding, achieving your goals and overcoming difficulties. Positive visualization can strengthen your determination and motivate you to act with confidence.

Discovering the inner courage to face challenges is an ongoing and challenging journey, but it's what makes us true heroes in our sales. Cultivating this courage allows us to surpass our own limits, achieve extraordinary results and inspire not only ourselves, but also our clients and teammates. Remember: courage is not an innate gift, but a skill that can be developed and honed. Embark on this journey of self-discovery, face your challenges bravely and become the hero of your own sales story.

The essential skills for success in sales

In sales, the difference between an ordinary salesperson and a true champion lies in the skills they develop and constantly improve throughout their careers. To achieve success and stand out in the competitive world of sales, it is essential to invest in training a comprehensive set of skills that go beyond product or service knowledge. In this chapter, we will explore some of the essential skills that every salesperson must develop in order to become a true sales hero.

Effective communication skills: the ability to communicate clearly, assertively and persuasively is the foundation of every successful salesperson. Mastering the art of communication allows you to establish an authentic connection with customers, convey your message convincingly and understand the needs and desires of the target audience. Listening attentively and knowing how to ask the right questions are also essential parts of this skill, as they demonstrate genuine interest in customers and help identify sales opportunities.

Empathy and emotional intelligence: developing empathy and emotional intelligence is crucial to becoming an exceptional salesperson. These skills allow you to understand customers' emotions and perspectives, adapting to their specific needs and showing genuine concern for helping them. Empathy is also key to handling objections and resolving conflicts sensitively and respectfully.

Negotiation and persuasion: being a good negotiator is one of the most valuable skills for any salesperson. The ability to negotiate skillfully allows you to reach agreements that are advantageous to both parties, creating a win-win scenario in negotiations. Knowing how to persuade customers ethically and convincingly is equally important, using solid arguments and clear benefits to arouse their interest and trust.

Time management and organization: in a dynamic and fast-paced sales environment, time management and organization are essential skills for maximizing productivity. Setting priorities, creating an efficient routine and using productivity tools help to optimize time and ensure that the most important activities are carried out at the right time.

Creative problem-solving: challenges are part of a salesperson's daily life, and the ability to solve problems creatively and effectively is crucial to overcoming them. Develop a solution-oriented mindset, looking for innovative alternatives and different approaches to deal with the challenges that come your way.

Self-confidence and resilience: self-confidence is based on in-depth knowledge of your product or service, as well as your sales skills. Believing in yourself is fundamental to facing rejections and challenges with resilience, as you will understand that every obstacle is an opportunity to learn and grow.

Establishing lasting relationships: one of the most valuable skills for a salesperson is the ability to establish and maintain lasting relationships with clients. Creating genuine bonds based on trust is the key to building loyalty and growing your customer network.

Continuous learning: finally, successful salespeople recognize that learning is a continuous process and are always looking to improve their skills and knowledge. Keep up to date with market trends, new sales techniques and personal development to remain competitive and prepared to face the challenges of the future.

Developing these essential skills is what makes a salesperson a true sales hero. Commitment to investing in the continuous improvement of your skills will make you stand out, conquer the market and achieve extraordinary results. Be the protagonist of your own sales journey, master these skills and write your success story as a true sales hero!

CHAPTER 2: THE POWER OF THE HEROIC MINDSET

The heroic mindset is the key that opens the door to success in sales and pushes us beyond the limits of the ordinary. This powerful mindset is what separates average salespeople from true champions, allowing the latter to face challenges with courage, determination and resilience. In this chapter, we'll explore the transformative power of the heroic mindset and how to cultivate it to become an exceptional salesperson.

Vision beyond the horizon: the heroic mindset enables us to see beyond the horizon and dream big. It inspires us to set ambitious goals and believe that we are capable of achieving them. The sales hero is not limited by current circumstances; they are driven by a clear and inspiring vision of what can be achieved in the future.

Overcoming limitations: one of the hallmarks of the heroic mentality is the ability to overcome limitations, whether internal or external. The sales hero doesn't let previous failures or limiting beliefs get him down. They believe in their potential and are willing to work hard to achieve success, even in the face of seemingly insurmountable challenges.

Acceptance of challenges: the sales hero doesn't run away from challenges; he embraces them wholeheartedly. The heroic mindset teaches us to see challenges as opportunities for growth and learning. Each obstacle is seen as a test of our courage and determination, and it is through these challenges that we become stronger and more prepared to face whatever lies ahead.

Unwavering resilience: resilience is an inherent characteristic of the heroic mindset. The heroic salesperson understands that ups and downs are part of the sales journey and that you have to persist even in the face of adversity. They pick themselves up after each fall, learn from their experiences and move forward with unwavering determination.

Focus on self-development: the hero mentality motivates us to constantly seek self-development. The sales hero is always looking to improve their skills, acquire new knowledge and grow both personally and professionally. They understand that in order to achieve extraordinary results, they need to be constantly evolving.

Responsibility and proactivity: the sales hero takes responsibility for their actions and results. They don't wait for favorable circumstances or ready-made solutions; instead, they take the initiative and actively seek ways to overcome challenges and achieve their goals. The heroic mindset teaches us that we are the creators of our own story and that we have the power to positively influence the course of our sales.

Gratitude and humility: despite his determination and ambition, the sales hero keeps gratitude and humility in his heart. He recognizes the importance of human connections, values every customer and teammate and shows appreciation for the opportunities that life and the sales career provide.

Inspiring others to success: the heroic mindset is not selfish; it inspires and motivates others to success. The sales hero seeks to share his knowledge and experience with teammates, enabling them to achieve extraordinary results too. They understand that their success is magnified when they help others on the road to success.

Cultivating the heroic mindset is an ongoing process that requires self-discipline and determination. By adopting this mindset, you become the protagonist of your own sales journey, facing challenges with courage, seeking constant growth and inspiring others to success. Remember: the heroic mindset is not exclusive to a privileged few, but is within the reach of every salesperson who is willing to embrace their inner courage and become a true sales hero.

The winning mentality to achieve audacious goals

A winning mindset is a determining factor for success in sales and for achieving audacious goals. It is the unshakeable belief that it is possible to overcome challenges, achieve extraordinary results and stand out as an exceptional salesperson. In this chapter, we'll explore how to adopt a winning mindset and how it can propel you to new heights of success in your sales career.

Believing in the possibility of success: the basis of a winning mindset is an unwavering belief in the possibility of success. A salesperson with a winning mindset believes that they are capable of achieving their goals, even if they seem challenging or distant. This belief strengthens their determination and drives them to persevere even in the face of obstacles.

Setting audacious goals: the winning mentality inspires us to set audacious and inspiring goals. The salesperson with this mindset understands that bold goals require extraordinary efforts, but also bring exceptional rewards. They are not afraid to dream big and draw up a detailed plan to achieve their boldest aspirations.

Turning obstacles into opportunities: while some may see obstacles as insurmountable barriers, the salesperson with a winning mentality sees them as opportunities to grow and excel. They learn from each challenge, use past experiences as a basis for new strategies and remain resilient even in the face of adversity.

Seeing failure as learning: the winning mentality allows salespeople to see failure as a learning opportunity. Instead of getting discouraged by rejections or unsatisfactory results, they analyze their actions, identify points for improvement and turn each experience into a springboard for future success.

Persistence and determination: the salesperson with a winning mentality has unshakeable determination. He doesn't give up at the first signs of difficulty; on the contrary, he persists with courage and optimism. Their resilience is fueled by a clear vision of their goals and the conviction that every effort counts towards achieving them.

Focus on solutions, not problems: while some focus on problems, the salesperson with a winning mentality focuses on solutions. They look for creative and proactive approaches to tackling challenges and finding opportunities for growth. This solution-oriented mindset makes him more effective and productive in his sales career.

Self-confidence and positive self-esteem: believing in yourself and cultivating a positive self-esteem are pillars of the winning mindset. Salespeople with this mindset recognize their abilities, value their achievements and remain confident even in times of uncertainty.

Search for continuous development: the winning mindset drives us to seek continuous development and improvement of our skills. Salespeople with this mindset are always looking for opportunities to learn, grow and excel in their field.

By adopting a winning mindset, you become the author of your own sales success story. This powerful mindset enables you to face challenges with confidence, pursue audacious results and inspire others with your determination and success. Remember that a winning mindset is not an innate trait, but a conscious choice that you can make at any time. Cultivate this mindset, stay focused on your goals and move towards success with the courage and determination of a true sales winner.

Overcoming the fear of rejection and adversity

The fear of rejection and adversity is one of the most significant barriers that salespeople face in their careers. This sense of fear can stem from past experiences, the fear of failure or not being well received by clients. However, overcoming this fear is essential to becoming a successful salesperson. In this chapter, we will explore powerful strategies for dealing with the fear of rejection and adversity, enabling you to face these challenges with courage and determination.

Recognizing the source of fear: the first step to overcoming the fear of rejection and adversity is to recognize its source. Understanding which experiences or beliefs are feeding this fear allows you to work towards overcoming it. Often, fear has its roots in past experiences that don't necessarily reflect present or future reality. By identifying these origins, you can begin to question their validity and take steps to address them.

Turning fear into motivation: a powerful approach to dealing with fear is to turn it into motivation. Instead of allowing fear to paralyze you, use it as a driving force to act with determination and proactivity. Visualize the positive results you can achieve if you overcome your fear, and keep this inspiring scenario in your mind as you prepare for your interactions with clients.

Practicing resilience: rejection and adversity are part of the sales journey. Understanding that not every situation will be successful is key to developing resilience. Resilience allows us to face setbacks with courage and learn from each experience. Instead of getting overwhelmed by rejection, use it as an opportunity to identify areas for improvement and grow as a salesperson.

Embracing authenticity: one of the greatest fears of salespeople is not being accepted or understood by customers. Authenticity is a powerful ally in overcoming this fear. By being genuine in your interactions with customers, you create a deeper and more authentic connection. Show yourself as a confident but also human professional, capable of understanding and relating to customers' needs and challenges.

Separating the "I" from the "No": it's important to separate rejection or adversity from your own personal valuations. Remember that when a customer rejects an offer or expresses objections, it is not a rejection of you as an individual. Instead of negatively internalizing negative responses, see them as part of the sales process and as opportunities to improve your approaches.

Adopting a learning mindset: Embracing a mindset of continuous learning is key to overcoming the fear of rejection and adversity. Every interaction with customers, whether successful or not, can provide valuable insights. View each experience as an opportunity to learn and grow, seeking to improve your skills and strategies with each new interaction.

Seeking support and feedback: Don't hesitate to seek support and feedback from teammates or mentors. Having someone to share your experiences and anxieties with can provide a valuable outside perspective and offer advice on how to deal with challenging situations. In addition, receiving constructive feedback allows you to identify areas for improvement and take steps to enhance your approach.

Celebrating your achievements: When facing the fear of rejection and adversity, it's important to remember your achievements. Celebrate each victory, however small, and recognize your continued progress. Cultivating a mindset of gratitude and appreciation for your achievements strengthens your self-esteem and confidence, which is essential for facing future challenges with more resilience.

Overcoming the fear of rejection and adversity is a process of self-discovery and self-development. Remember that it's normal to feel fear in some situations, but what matters is how you decide to face it. Cultivate inner courage, trust in your abilities and embrace every challenge as an opportunity to grow and become an even more exceptional salesperson. With dedication and determination, you can overcome fear and achieve extraordinary results in your sales career.

CHAPTER 3: THE CUSTOMER AND HERO'S JOURNEY

Like the heroes of legends and mythologies, customers embark on a journey full of challenges, discoveries and transformations throughout their shopping experience. The salesperson, in turn, plays a crucial role in this journey, taking on the role of the customer's guide and ally in the quest for success. In this chapter, we will explore the fascinating analogy between the customer journey and the hero's journey, understanding how salespeople can become true heroes for their customers and lead them to success.

The call to adventure: just as the hero is summoned to a life-changing adventure, the customer also faces a call to action when they perceive a need or desire to be met. At this point, the salesperson plays the role of mentor, presenting solutions and awakening the customer's awareness of the opportunity at hand.

Knowledge of the unknown: as the hero sets off on his journey, he faces the unknown and enters uncharted territory. The customer, when considering the purchase, may feel insecure or anxious about the decisions to be made. At this stage, the salesperson plays the role of guide, providing detailed information, clarifying doubts and demonstrating the value of the product or service.

Facing challenges and obstacles: during their journey, the hero faces challenges and obstacles that test their courage and determination. In the same way, the customer may encounter objections, financial concerns or doubts about the viability of the purchase. The salesperson, as an ally, must help the customer overcome these challenges by offering persuasive arguments, creative solutions and showing empathy to understand and resolve their concerns.

Transformation and growth: as the hero faces the challenges and learns valuable lessons, he undergoes a personal transformation and grows as an individual. In the same way, the customer's journey is marked by an evolution, as they search for a solution that satisfies their needs and aspirations. The salesperson at this stage must be able to adapt to the customer's pace, understand their changing perspectives and adjust their approach as the journey progresses.

The triumphant return: after achieving their goals and overcoming challenges, the hero returns triumphant, transformed by their journey. For the customer, the moment of closing the purchase represents their own victory, the achievement of a solution that meets their expectations and needs. At this stage, the salesperson celebrates with the customer, reinforcing the value of the decision made and ensuring that the after-sales service is just as exceptional.

The hero's legacy: in mythology, heroes leave a legacy that inspires future generations. In the same way, the satisfied customer becomes a source of reference for other potential customers, sharing their positive experience and recommending the salesperson as a true sales hero. The salesperson then understands that their journey as a guide and ally doesn't end with the sale, but is a continuous journey of loyalty and building lasting relationships.

By understanding the customer's journey from the hero's perspective, the salesperson places themselves in the role of protagonist in the sales narrative, with the responsibility of guiding, supporting and offering solutions that transform the customer's journey into a success story. The journey of the customer and the hero is an exciting and inspiring parable for all salespeople, demonstrating the importance of becoming a true hero for customers, leading them with courage, empathy and excellence to achieve their goals and build a lasting partnership.

Mapping the customer journey to create genuine connections

One of the keys to becoming an exceptional salesperson is to understand the customer journey in its entirety. Mapping this journey is a powerful strategy that allows salespeople to create genuine and meaningful connections with their customers, establishing a relationship of trust and empathy throughout the buying process. In this chapter, we'll explore how to map the customer journey and how to use this knowledge to build long-lasting and successful relationships.

The first contact: mapping the customer journey begins with the first contact between the customer and the salesperson. It is at this crucial moment that the salesperson must show genuine interest in the customer, listen carefully to their needs and concerns, and lay the foundations for a relationship of trust from the outset. The focus should be on understanding the customer's expectations and how the salesperson can add value to their specific needs.

Research and discovery: in this stage, the salesperson delves deeper into researching and discovering the customer's needs and challenges. This involves asking intelligent questions, exploring the customer's motivations and identifying opportunities to offer customized solutions. The salesperson must be prepared to listen empathetically, understand the customer's perspective and present relevant information that meets their specific demands.

Identifying solutions: based on the information gathered, the salesperson must identify the best solutions for the customer's needs. It is essential to present clear and transparent options, highlighting the benefits and advantages of each proposed solution. By demonstrating an understanding of the customer's needs, the salesperson strengthens the bond of trust and shows that they are genuinely interested in offering the best possible solution.

The buying experience: the customer journey is not limited to the sale itself, but includes the entire buying experience. The salesperson must ensure that the customer experience is positive and memorable at every point of contact, from the presentation of the solutions to the after-sales service. Each interaction must reflect the salesperson's dedication to providing an exceptional experience and align with the customer's values and expectations.

Follow-up and ongoing relationship: mapping the customer journey doesn't end with the sale; it includes follow-up and ongoing relationship. The salesperson must remain present in the customer's life, ensuring that their needs are being met and that they are satisfied with the solution they have acquired. Maintaining proactive and genuine communication helps build a deeper connection and strengthens the relationship of trust over time.

Anticipating and exceeding expectations: one of the best ways to create genuine connections is to anticipate and exceed the customer's expectations. A salesperson who is proactive and attentive to the customer's needs demonstrates that they are truly committed to offering the best possible service. Surprising the customer with exceptional service, personalized solutions and genuine care creates a lasting positive impression and builds long-term customer loyalty.

Feedback and learning: mapping the customer journey is a continuous journey of learning and improvement. The salesperson must seek feedback and evaluations from the customer in order to understand how they can improve and adjust their strategies according to their constantly evolving needs. This valuable feedback is a source of insights for improving the customer experience and strengthening genuine connections.

By mapping the customer journey, the salesperson puts themselves in the customer's shoes, understanding their needs, challenges and aspirations. This customer-centered approach allows the salesperson to create genuine and meaningful connections based on empathy, trust and mutual understanding. The customer journey is an opportunity for the salesperson to become a true ally and guide for their customers, providing personalized solutions and an exceptional buying experience.

With this approach, the salesperson stands out as an exceptional professional, building lasting and successful relationships that go beyond the simple commercial transaction.

Being the guide customers need to find solutions

In the world of sales, customers often face a sea of options, complex decisions and doubts about which path to follow to achieve their goals. In this context, the salesperson's role as a guide is essential to help them navigate this journey and find the best solutions for their needs. In this chapter, we'll explore how salespeople can become trusted and empowered guides, offering support, knowledge and guidance to customers so that they can find the ideal solutions.

Understanding the customer's needs: the first step to being an effective guide is to truly understand the customer's needs. This involves listening carefully to their demands, asking clear and empathetic questions and analyzing their expectations and objectives. The more the salesperson knows about the customer, the more accurate their guidance and indication of appropriate solutions will be.

Knowledge and product mastery: to be a reliable guide, salespeople must have a solid grasp of their knowledge and the products or services they offer. It is essential to be up-to-date on the latest trends, features and benefits of the solutions available. In this way, the salesperson can provide accurate and relevant information, making it easier for the customer to make a decision.

Presenting clear and personalized options: a skilled guide offers clear and personalized options that meet the customer's specific needs. Each customer is unique, and the salesperson must be able to adapt their recommendations based on individual preferences, budget and goals. By presenting tailor-made options, the salesperson demonstrates that they are genuinely committed to finding the best solution for each customer.

Clarifying doubts and objections: during the customer journey, it is natural for doubts and objections to arise about the options presented. The attentive guide is dedicated to clarifying all questions, providing additional information, showing concrete evidence and offering persuasive arguments. They address objections empathetically, showing understanding and providing solutions that eliminate the client's concerns.

Providing impartial guidance: a true guide is impartial in their guidance, focusing on the client's interest above all else. He doesn't push unnecessary or inappropriate solutions just to close a sale. On the contrary, they are transparent and honest, highlighting the pros and cons of each option and allowing the customer to make the best decision for their needs.

Building trust and rapport: trust is the basis of the relationship between the guide and the client. The salesperson must act with integrity, delivering what they promise, meeting deadlines and delivering results. In addition, they make themselves accessible and available to the client at all stages of the journey, demonstrating that they are committed to providing ongoing support.

Helping with implementation and after-sales: the guide doesn't abandon the client after the sale has been made. They accompany the customer through the implementation of the solution, ensuring that everything runs smoothly and successfully. They also keep in touch after the sale, seeking feedback and offering additional assistance if necessary. This accompaniment reinforces the guide's value as a reliable partner and demonstrates that they are truly committed to the customer's success.

Being the guide customers need to find solutions is a continuous journey of learning, empathy and dedication. The salesperson who positions themselves as a guide builds lasting and meaningful relationships, earning customer loyalty and creating a competitive edge in the industry. By offering genuine support, knowledge and guidance, the skilled guide helps customers on the path to success, becoming a valuable and reliable ally on their journey towards achieving their goals.

CHAPTER 4: THE HERO IN THE SALES APPROACH

In the world of sales, the salesperson plays an essential role as the hero of the narrative, guiding customers on their journey towards achieving their goals and needs. Like the heroes of legend, the salesperson faces challenges, seeks creative solutions and takes responsibility for delivering exceptional service. In this chapter, we will explore the importance of the hero in the sales approach and how the hero's attributes can be used to create genuine connections and achieve extraordinary results.

Courage for the first step: just as the hero faces the call to adventure, the salesperson demonstrates courage when taking the first step in the sales approach. They overcome any initial hesitations, trust in their abilities and make themselves available to help the customer. The salesperson's courage in initiating the sales process is key to establishing an initial connection and paving the way for building a meaningful relationship.

Empathy and understanding: the hero not only faces challenges, but also understands the needs and concerns of those he protects. In the same way, salespeople must be empathetic and understanding with customers, listening carefully to their demands and trying to see the world from their perspective. Empathy allows the salesperson to create a personalized approach and offer solutions that truly meet the customer's needs.

Determination to overcome obstacles: the hero's path is full of obstacles, and salespeople also encounter challenges on their sales journey. Determination is essential for overcoming objections, circumventing setbacks and persisting even in the face of difficulties. Determined salespeople don't get down on themselves and see every challenge as an opportunity to improve their skills and strategies.

Creativity in problem-solving: the hero often needs to find creative solutions to deal with adverse situations. In the same way, the creative salesperson is able to identify personalized and innovative solutions to meet the customer's needs. They are willing to think outside the box, adapt to circumstances and offer options that stand out in the market.

Responsibility and commitment: just as the hero takes on the responsibility of protecting and guiding others, the salesperson also takes on the commitment of offering exceptional service and quality solutions. The salesperson's responsibility is to honor their promises, meet deadlines and ensure that the client's expectations are met.

Resilience in the face of adversity: the hero faces moments of adversity, but his resilience keeps him persevering in his mission. The resilient salesperson is not shaken by rejections or temporary failures, but finds the strength to move on and learn from each experience. Resilience is a valuable attribute that enables salespeople to stand out and achieve exceptional results.

Celebrating achievements: the hero celebrates his victories, and salespeople should also celebrate their achievements when they close a sale or achieve significant results. Celebrating not only reinforces the salesperson's motivation, but also shows the customer that they are valued and that the partnership is worthy of celebration.

The customer's ally and guide: the true hero is not just a savior, but an ally and guide to those he protects. In the same way, salespeople position themselves as reliable allies and guides for their customers. They are present throughout the customer journey, offering support, knowledge and assistance at every stage.

By incorporating the hero's attributes into their sales approach, salespeople stand out as exceptional professionals, capable of creating genuine connections and achieving outstanding results. They don't just sell products or services, they act as a guide to help customers achieve their goals and find successful, personalized solutions. With courage, empathy, determination and creativity, the salesperson takes on the role of the hero of the sales narrative, leaving a lasting impression and building trusting relationships with customers.

Creating a striking and lasting first impression

The first impression is a crucial moment in the sales journey. It is in this initial moment that the salesperson has the opportunity to make a positive impact and win the customer's attention. A striking and lasting first impression is the key to establishing a meaningful connection from the outset, which can make all the difference in building a solid and successful relationship. In this chapter, we'll explore powerful strategies for creating a first impression that lasts in the customer's mind and opens the door to a successful partnership.

Wearing the armor of trust: trust is one of the fundamental pillars of a positive first impression. Salespeople must wear the armor of confidence, presenting themselves with assertive posture and body language. A professional appearance and a firm handshake convey to the customer that the salesperson is trustworthy and capable of keeping their promises.

The importance of empathy: the customer needs to feel that they are being listened to and understood from the very first moment. Empathy is an essential skill for creating this emotional connection. The salesperson must show genuine interest in the customer's needs, asking relevant questions and being willing to understand their unique perspective.

Master the art of communication: clear and effective communication is essential for making a good impression. Salespeople must speak confidently and articulately, avoiding jargon or excessive technical language. Communicating assertively and persuasively demonstrates to the customer that the salesperson has mastery of the subject and can provide valuable information.

Smile and be charismatic: a genuine smile is a powerful tool for creating a positive first impression. It conveys friendliness, charisma and a welcoming atmosphere. A charismatic salesperson is able to captivate the customer and make the interaction more pleasant, making it easier to open up to dialogue and explore the customer's needs.

Personalize the approach: each customer is unique, and a personalized approach shows the customer that the salesperson values their individuality. Knowing the customer by name and mentioning relevant details about your company or history creates an atmosphere of trust and makes the customer feel special and attended to in an exclusive way.

Offer value right from the start: an outstanding first impression goes beyond a simple greeting. The salesperson must be able to offer value right from the start, presenting information or insights that are relevant and useful to the customer. Sharing valuable knowledge and being willing to help from the very first contact sets the tone for a relationship of trust and reciprocity.

Listen more than you talk: a lasting first impression is also the result of active listening. Salespeople should spend more time listening to the customer than talking about themselves or their products. This allows the salesperson to understand the customer's needs and identify the best solutions, demonstrating that they are genuinely interested in helping the customer, not just making a sale.

Show enthusiasm and passion: enthusiasm is contagious and creates a positive atmosphere. Salespeople must show passion for what they do and the solutions they offer. Conveying enthusiasm is a powerful way of arousing the customer's interest and demonstrating that the salesperson believes in the value of what they are offering.

Creating a striking and lasting first impression requires a careful balance between interpersonal skills, product knowledge and authenticity. The salesperson who presents themselves with confidence, empathy, effective communication and a healthy dose of charisma creates a solid foundation for building a meaningful relationship with the customer. A positive first impression is not just a starting point; it is the foundation for a successful partnership and for winning the customer's trust in the long term.

Using stories and narratives to engage customers

Stories have been a powerful communication tool throughout human history. Since time immemorial, narratives have been used to convey knowledge, values, emotions and teachings. In the context of sales, stories play a key role in engaging customers in a meaningful way, making the approach more memorable, emotional and persuasive. In this chapter, we will explore the art of using stories and narratives to create authentic connections with customers and enhance the power of persuasion in sales.

The science of stories: stories have a solid scientific basis for engaging human beings. Studies show that when we listen to stories, our brains release hormones such as oxytocin, which make us feel more connected and empathetic to the characters in the story. By using narratives in sales, salespeople can activate this emotional response in customers, creating a deep and lasting connection.

Captivating characters and journeys: every good story has captivating characters and engaging journeys. In the context of sales, the customer is the hero of the story, and the salesperson is the guide who helps them on their journey to success. By creating narratives that place the customer as the protagonist, the salesperson can arouse the customer's interest and generate empathy with their situation and needs.

Demonstrating value with success stories: success stories are a powerful way of demonstrating the value of the solutions offered. By sharing cases of previous customers who have achieved positive results thanks to the product or service, the salesperson shows the customer that the proposed solutions really work in practice. These authentic and real stories increase the salesperson's credibility and give the customer a concrete vision of the benefits they can obtain.

Involving the customer in an interactive narrative: an interactive narrative involves the customer in a continuous and stimulating dialog. The salesperson can ask questions that lead the customer to become emotionally involved in the story and to visualize how the proposed solution can meet their needs. This engaging approach makes the customer an active part of the narrative, increasing their interest and engagement.

Emotion as a persuasive tool: stories have the power to evoke emotions in listeners. The salesperson can use this emotion strategically to persuade the customer to make a decision. By creating stories that arouse positive emotions such as joy, hope and satisfaction, the salesperson can associate these feelings with the solution being offered, making it more attractive and desirable for the customer.

Cultural connections and shared values: stories that address cultural themes or values shared by the salesperson and the customer have an even greater impact. These narratives create a deep emotional connection, as they demonstrate that the salesperson understands and identifies with the customer's beliefs and challenges. This affinity can be a decisive factor in the customer's choice for a lasting partnership.

Create a persuasive narrative arc: an effective story has a persuasive narrative arc, with an engaging introduction, an exciting development and a satisfying conclusion. The salesperson must structure their narrative in such a way as to attract the customer's attention right from the start, develop a plot that keeps them interested and conclude with a persuasive and clear call to action.

Stories that inspire and motivate: the best stories are those that inspire and motivate the customer to act. The salesperson can use narratives that show how other companies or people have overcome similar challenges and achieved exceptional results. These inspiring stories motivate the customer to believe that they too can achieve success with the help of the salesperson and the solutions proposed.

By using stories and narratives in their sales approaches, the salesperson not only makes the experience more engaging, but also establishes an emotional and authentic connection with the customer. Stories allow the salesperson to communicate information in a more memorable way, create empathy and influence the customer's decisions in a persuasive way. By incorporating the art of storytelling into their sales strategy, salespeople elevate their approach to a more human and meaningful level, building solid and lasting relationships with customers.

Using stories and narratives as a powerful sales tool is a skill that can be mastered with practice and refinement. By recognizing the emotional power of stories, salespeople can create authentic connections with customers, providing a more personalized and meaningful buying experience. The science behind stories reveals that they have the ability to influence customer decisions in a unique way, activating emotional responses that drive action and decision-making.

By telling success stories, salespeople can demonstrate the effectiveness of their solutions in a tangible and concrete way, connecting the benefits offered with the customer's specific needs. Interactive interaction with the customer allows the narrative to be shaped according to the customer's responses and reactions, making it even more engaging and relevant. The strategic use of emotion in stories can influence the customer's perception of the proposed solution, generating enthusiasm, trust and a stronger emotional connection.

Building narratives that connect with the cultural and shared values between the salesperson and the customer reinforces the feeling of affinity and mutual understanding, increasing the salesperson's trust and credibility. The well-structured narrative arc allows the story to be told in a compelling way, capturing the customer's attention from the beginning to the final call to action.

As well as persuading the customer to make a decision, stories also have the power to inspire and motivate. By sharing narratives of overcoming and success, the salesperson encourages the customer to believe that they too can achieve exceptional results with the help of the proposed solutions.

Therefore, mastering the art of using stories and narratives in sales is a valuable skill that allows the salesperson to create a genuine emotional connection with the customer, making the buying experience more memorable, relevant and persuasive. By incorporating authentic and inspiring stories into their sales approaches, salespeople stand out as professionals capable of creating solid, long-term relationships with customers, achieving exceptional results and building a positive reputation in the market. The art of storytelling is a powerful tool that allows salespeople to elevate their approach to a more human, empathetic and effective level, earning the trust and loyalty of customers over time.

CHAPTER 5: TACKLING THE VILLAINS OF SALES

Just as in epic stories, the world of sales also has its villains who can hinder the salesperson's path to success. These "sales villains" are obstacles and challenges that can sabotage a salesperson's efforts and prevent them from closing deals. In this chapter, we will explore the main villains that salespeople face on a daily basis and present effective strategies for overcoming them and achieving extraordinary results.

Resistance to change: Resistance to change is a powerful villain that can arise in both customers and sales teams. Customers are often used to their current routines and solutions, making it difficult to persuade them to consider new alternatives. To tackle this villain, the salesperson must clearly communicate the benefits of the proposed solutions, highlighting how they can overcome current challenges and drive growth.

Fear of rejection: fear of rejection is a villain that can undermine the salesperson's confidence and affect their sales approach. It's natural for salespeople to face negatives, but overcoming the fear of rejection is essential to persisting and achieving success. Salespeople should see rejections as opportunities to learn and improve, seeking constructive feedback to improve their strategies.

Lack of differentiation: the lack of differentiation is a villain that can make the salesperson's products and services unattractive in the eyes of the customer. To face this challenge, salespeople must highlight the unique differentials of their solutions, showing how they stand out from the competition and offer additional value to the customer.

Fierce competition: fierce competition is a villain that can make the market challenging and competitive. The salesperson must study the competition in depth, identifying its strengths and weaknesses. This analysis allows the salesperson to position their solutions strategically, highlighting the benefits that make them the best choice for the customer.

Customer procrastination: customer procrastination can be a villain that prolongs the sales cycle and makes it difficult to close the deal. The salesperson must demonstrate a sense of urgency and offer incentives to encourage the customer to make a quick decision. In addition, the salesperson can proactively follow up with the customer, offering support and additional information to help them make their decision.

Lack of trust: lack of trust is a villain that can compromise the salesperson's credibility with the customer. To face this challenge, salespeople must be transparent and honest in their interactions, keeping their promises and establishing a relationship of mutual trust. Success stories and references from satisfied customers can also strengthen confidence in the solution offered.

Misalignment with the customer's needs: not fully understanding the customer's needs is a villain that can lead salespeople to offer inadequate solutions. The salesperson must take the time to listen carefully to the customer, asking the right questions and trying to understand their demands and challenges. Based on this knowledge, the salesperson can adapt their strategies to meet the customer's specific needs.

Complacency and stagnation: complacency and stagnation are villains that can limit growth and innovation in the sales field. To deal with them, salespeople must always seek continuous improvement, looking for new strategies, learning from past experiences and keeping up to date with market trends.

Facing the villains of sales requires determination, creativity and courage. The salesperson who remains resilient in the face of challenges, learns from adversity and adopts intelligent and differentiated strategies has the power to turn villains into allies. By overcoming these obstacles with a strategic approach and a growth mindset, the salesperson achieves exceptional results and becomes a true sales hero. Remember: every challenge overcome is an opportunity for growth and improvement, and the salesperson's journey to success is a story full of learning and achievement. Face the villains of sales with courage and determination, and write the successful chapter of your career as a salesperson!

In this chapter, we explore some of the main villains that salespeople face in the world of sales, as well as effective strategies for overcoming them. Each of these villains can represent a unique challenge, but with a strategic approach and a growth mindset, salespeople can turn them into opportunities for growth and success.

When facing resistance to change, the salesperson must focus on communicating the benefits of the proposed solutions, highlighting how they can overcome the customer's current challenges and drive growth. Dealing with the fear of rejection requires persistence and confidence, seeing negatives as opportunities to learn and improve.

Lack of differentiation can be overcome by highlighting the unique differentials of the solutions offered, making them more attractive in the eyes of the customer. In the face of fierce competition, salespeople must study the competition in detail, identifying strengths and weaknesses in order to position their solutions strategically.

To overcome customer procrastination, the salesperson must demonstrate a sense of urgency and offer incentives that encourage the customer to make a quick decision. In addition, proactive follow-up can provide the necessary support to help the customer with their decision.

Lack of trust can be combated by being transparent, keeping promises and establishing a relationship of mutual trust with the customer. The salesperson can also use success stories and references from satisfied customers to reinforce confidence in the solution offered.

It is essential that the salesperson is aligned with the customer's needs, listening carefully to their demands and challenges and adapting their strategies to meet them. In addition, complacency and stagnation can be overcome through continuous improvement, learning and the search for new strategies and market trends.

Tackling the villains of sales requires courage, determination and creativity. Every challenge overcome is an opportunity for growth and improvement, and salespeople who remain resilient in the face of adversity can turn these obstacles into allies on their journey to success.

Remember that a salesperson's journey is a story of learning and achievement. By facing the villains of sales with courage and determination, salespeople can become true sales heroes, achieving exceptional results and leaving a lasting impression on their customers. With a strategic approach, a growth mindset and the determination to excel in the world of sales, salespeople can write the successful chapter of their career, overcoming the villains and achieving extraordinary results.

Identifying and overcoming common obstacles in the sales process

A salesperson's journey is full of challenges and obstacles that can hinder the sales process. In this chapter, we will explore the most common obstacles faced by salespeople and provide effective strategies for identifying and overcoming them. By understanding these challenges and learning how to get around them, salespeople can improve their approach, increase their efficiency and achieve exceptional results.

Identifying gatekeepers: gatekeepers are responsible for filtering access to decision-makers in companies. Identifying them and overcoming their barriers is essential to reaching the key decision-makers. The salesperson must develop persuasive communication techniques and strategies to build relationships with these gatekeepers, gaining their trust and access to key decision-makers.

Dealing with competition: fierce competition is a constant obstacle in the sales process. The salesperson must be prepared to face the competition strategically, highlighting the unique differentials of their solutions and demonstrating the additional value they offer the customer. A thorough understanding of the competition's strengths and weaknesses is fundamental to positioning yourself advantageously in the market.

Bypassing customer resistance: customer resistance can arise at various stages of the sales process, whether due to fear of change or lack of understanding of the value of the solution offered. The salesperson must practice empathy, listen carefully to the customer's objections and offer convincing answers, highlighting how the proposed solution can meet the customer's specific needs.

Managing the sales cycle: the sales cycle can be complex and time-consuming, requiring patience and organization on the part of the salesperson. It is essential to manage the sales process efficiently, monitoring each stage and offering proactive support to the client. The use of sales tools and technologies can also optimize the process and increase productivity.

Overcoming a lack of engagement: in some cases, customers may not show enough interest or engagement in the sales process. The salesperson must seek to involve the customer more actively, creating a personalized approach that is relevant to their needs. The use of engaging stories and narratives can also captivate the customer and make the buying experience more attractive.

Dealing with the customer's changing priorities: the customer's priorities can change over time, impacting their purchasing decisions. The salesperson must keep up to date with the customer's needs and adapt their approach accordingly. Flexibility and the ability to adjust sales strategies are key to keeping up with constantly evolving demands.

Overcoming the fear of negotiating: the negotiation process can generate anxiety and insecurity in some salespeople. Overcoming the fear of negotiating requires confidence in your abilities, in-depth knowledge of the product or service on offer and a collaborative mindset to find solutions that meet the interests of both parties.

Generating qualified leads: generating qualified leads is a challenge for many salespeople. To overcome it, salespeople must use effective marketing and prospecting strategies to identify and attract potential customers who are aligned with the ideal customer profile. Nurturing leads and building relationships are essential for turning leads into business opportunities.

Staying motivated: the sales journey can be full of ups and downs, which can affect the salesperson's motivation. It's important to develop a positive mindset, set realistic goals and celebrate every achievement, no matter how small. The support of teammates and leaders can also be a valuable source of motivation and encouragement.

Learning from experiences: every obstacle faced in the sales process is an opportunity to learn and grow. Salespeople should analyze their experiences, identify points for improvement and apply these learnings to their future approach. The continuous search for improvement and the willingness to face challenges are essential traits of the sales hero.

Overcoming common obstacles in the sales process requires dedication, strategic skills and a resilient mindset. By proactively identifying and tackling these challenges, salespeople can turn obstacles into opportunities, building lasting relationships with customers and achieving exceptional results. Remember that the salesperson's journey is a story of continuous learning and growth, and each overcoming is an achievement that makes you stronger and more skillful in your path as a sales hero.

Strategies for dealing with objections and adversity

In the world of sales, objections and adversity are inevitable. However, these challenges can be transformed into opportunities to strengthen the relationship with the customer and boost sales success. In this chapter, we will explore effective strategies for dealing with objections with confidence, overcoming adversity with resilience and winning the customer's trust, emerging as true sales heroes.

Understanding the customer's objections: the first step in dealing with objections is to understand the customer's concerns and hesitations in an empathetic way. The salesperson must listen carefully to the customer, asking clear questions to identify the reasons behind the objections. By understanding the customer's concerns, the salesperson can offer more precise and relevant answers, showing that they are genuinely interested in solving their problems.

Preparing for common objections: preparation is the key to overcoming objections with confidence. The salesperson should anticipate common objections related to the product, price, delivery time or other aspects relevant to the customer. By being prepared for these objections, the salesperson can provide solid, convincing answers and avoid being caught off guard.

Turning objections into opportunities: objections can be seen as opportunities to offer the customer more information and highlight the benefits of your solution. By approaching objections with empathy and respect, the salesperson can create a collaborative environment for exploring the customer's concerns, overcoming their hesitations and offering personalized solutions.

Using social proof: social proof, such as testimonials from satisfied customers and successful case studies, is valuable for gaining the customer's trust and overcoming objections. The salesperson should use success stories and tangible evidence to demonstrate the effectiveness of their solutions and show how they can solve the customer's specific challenges.

Demonstrating knowledge and expertise: the customer's trust is essential for overcoming objections. The salesperson must demonstrate their knowledge and expertise in the market and industry, providing valuable information and relevant insights that add value to the customer's decision. By showing themselves to be a reliable expert, the salesperson increases the likelihood that the customer will trust their recommendations.

Adopting a personalized approach: every customer is unique, and a personalized approach is key to dealing with objections effectively. The salesperson must listen to each customer's specific needs and concerns, adapting their responses and solutions accordingly. A personalized approach shows the customer that their concerns are taken seriously and that they are valued as an individual.

Overcoming adversity with resilience: in addition to objections, salespeople can face adversity throughout their journey. Resilience is the ability to adapt and overcome these adversities with determination and courage. Salespeople must learn from the challenges they face, seeking creative solutions and maintaining a positive attitude to move forward, even in the face of difficulties.

Learning from previous experiences: every objection overcome and adversity faced is a learning opportunity. Salespeople should reflect on their previous experiences, identifying strengths and areas for improvement in their sales approach. Continuous learning is essential for professional improvement and for becoming a more capable and efficient sales hero.

Building long-term relationships: by overcoming objections and adversity, the salesperson can strengthen the relationship with the customer. An honest and empathetic approach, combined with a genuine commitment to meeting the customer's needs, can create a solid foundation for a lasting and productive relationship.

Celebrating achievements: every objection overcome and every adversity faced are achievements that should be celebrated. Salespeople should recognize their victories, even the small ones, and celebrate every advance in their sales journey. Celebrating achievements strengthens motivation and boosts confidence to face new challenges.

Dealing with objections and adversity requires strategic skills, empathy and resilience. By understanding the customer's objections, being prepared to face them, using social proof and demonstrating expertise, the salesperson can overcome objections with confidence and win the customer's trust. Facing adversity with resilience, learning from previous experiences and building solid relationships with customers are essential ingredients for becoming a sales hero and achieving extraordinary results. The salesperson's journey is a story full of challenges, learnings and achievements, and every step taken towards success contributes to building a career of excellence in sales. Remember that perseverance and commitment to facing objections and adversity are the hallmarks of a true sales hero.

CHAPTER 6: THE TOOLS OF THE SALES HERO

In the modern world of sales, success requires the efficient use of tools and technologies that enhance the effectiveness of the salesperson. In this chapter, we will explore the main tools of the sales hero, highlighting how they can optimize the sales process, improve productivity and strengthen the connection with customers. By mastering these tools, salespeople can stand out in a competitive market and achieve extraordinary results.

CRM (Customer Relationship Management): CRM is one of the most powerful tools for the sales hero. It enables efficient management of customer data, interaction history, follow-ups and pending tasks. With a well-used CRM, salespeople can follow the customer journey, create closer relationships and offer personalized service, identifying business opportunities and building customer loyalty.

Marketing automation and email marketing: marketing automation and email marketing are fundamental resources for generating and nurturing leads. These tools allow salespeople to send relevant and personalized content to customers at strategic times, keeping them engaged and nurturing the relationship over time. Marketing automation also helps identify qualified leads, allowing salespeople to dedicate their time to the most promising prospects.

Video and web conferencing platforms: video and web conferencing platforms have become essential for the sales hero, especially in a remote sales scenario. With these tools, salespeople can hold virtual meetings with customers anywhere in the world, building more personal and human relationships, even at a distance. Video presentations also allow salespeople to create a more significant and memorable impact.

Social networks and social selling: social networks offer a vast field of opportunities for the sales hero. Social selling involves the strategic use of social networks to connect with potential customers, build authority and influence in the market, and share relevant content that attracts qualified leads. Salespeople can use social media to create a strong personal brand and position themselves as experts in their field.

Data analysis platforms: the sales hero must make decisions based on concrete data. Data analysis platforms offer valuable insights into customer behavior, the performance of sales strategies and market trends. This information allows salespeople to adjust their approach according to customer needs and identify opportunities for growth.

Sales automation tools: sales automation tools help salespeople optimize repetitive and administrative processes, saving time and increasing efficiency. They can include anything from email scheduling to automatic lead follow-up. By automating routine tasks, salespeople can focus on more strategic activities that require direct interaction with the customer.

E-commerce and e-business platforms: for salespeople working in digital environments, e-commerce and e-business platforms are essential for facilitating the online sales process. These tools allow salespeople to make their products or services available in a practical and secure way, as well as offering customers a pleasant shopping experience.

Productivity apps: Productivity apps help sales heroes organize their work, keep track of goals, schedule tasks and optimize their day-to-day lives. From project management apps to time tracking apps, these tools help salespeople stay focused and maintain the discipline needed to achieve their goals.

Gamification tools: gamification is a fun and effective approach to motivating the sales team and achieving goals. Gamification tools encourage salespeople to achieve certain goals through healthy competitions, prizes and rewards, creating a stimulating and productive environment.

Sales and performance analysis software: for the sales hero, measuring performance is essential for continuous improvement. Sales analysis software allows salespeople to monitor key performance indicators, evaluate their results and identify areas that need improvement. These tools help salespeople make informed decisions and improve their sales approach.

By mastering the tools of the sales hero, professionals can improve their skills, optimize the sales process and build lasting relationships with customers. By using these tools strategically, salespeople become more agile, efficient and proactive on their journey to success. The true sales hero knows that knowledge and intelligent use of the available tools are key to standing out in a competitive market and achieving exceptional results. With an innovative approach, combined with the use of the best tools available, the salesperson can create a significant impact and become a true sales hero.

Mastering persuasion and negotiation techniques

Persuasion and negotiation are essential skills for the sales hero. Mastering these techniques is key to winning the customer's trust, overcoming objections and successfully closing deals. In this chapter, we will explore effective strategies for improving persuasion and negotiation skills, enabling salespeople to achieve exceptional results and establish lasting relationships with clients.

Understanding the psychology of persuasion: persuasion is an art based on understanding human psychology. The sales hero must learn to identify customers' emotional triggers and use persuasive arguments that resonate with their needs and desires. The use of social proof, authority, scarcity and other principles of persuasion can make the salesperson's offers more attractive and convincing.

Creating a persuasive message: persuasive communication is key to gaining the customer's attention and interest. The salesperson must learn to convey their message clearly, concisely and convincingly, highlighting the unique benefits of their solution and demonstrating how it can solve the customer's specific problems. The use of stories and practical examples can make the message more engaging and memorable.

Developing empathy and active listening: empathy is the key to establishing genuine connections with customers. The sales hero must listen attentively to the customer's needs and concerns, showing genuine interest in their stories and challenges. Active listening allows the salesperson to identify opportunities to personalize their sales approach and offer solutions that are more in line with the customer's expectations.

Identifying the customer's pain points: to persuade effectively, the salesperson must identify the customer's pain points and highlight how their solution can alleviate these problems. A thorough understanding of the challenges faced by the customer allows the salesperson to adapt their message and arguments to show how their offer can have a positive impact and bring real results.

Negotiating with strategic techniques: negotiation is an art that requires strategic skills and the ability to deal with concessions. The sales hero must be prepared to negotiate collaboratively, seeking solutions that meet the interests of both parties. The ability to create value during the negotiation is essential to ensure that the client realizes the cost-benefit of the offer presented.

Overcoming objections with persuasion: when facing objections, the salesperson must use persuasive techniques to respond clearly and convincingly, converting concerns into opportunities. Using examples of satisfied customers, case studies and measurable results can reinforce the salesperson's credibility and show how their solution has already been successful in similar situations.

Finding win-win solutions: the sales hero must look for win-win solutions, i.e. agreements that benefit both the customer and the company. By finding a balance point that meets the customer's needs and sales targets, the salesperson builds a relationship based on trust and mutual collaboration.

Dealing with difficult negotiating tactics: during the negotiation, the salesperson may encounter difficult tactics from the customer. Learning to identify and deal with these tactics, such as exaggerated demands, repetitive objections or pressure for discounts, is essential to keeping calm and conducting the negotiation assertively.

Using body language to your advantage: body language is a powerful tool for persuasion. The sales hero must pay attention to their posture, facial expressions and gestures, ensuring that their body language conveys confidence and security. In addition, learning to read the customer's body language can provide valuable insights into their reactions and intentions during the negotiation.

Learning from every experience: persuasion and negotiation are skills that can be honed with continuous practice. The sales hero must learn from each sales experience, analyzing their approaches, identifying strengths and areas for improvement, and constantly seeking professional improvement.

Persuasion and negotiation are arts that can be developed with dedication and knowledge. The sales hero who masters these techniques can build trusting relationships, overcome challenges and achieve sales success. The combination of persuasive communication, empathy, strategic negotiation skills and reading body language can boost a salesperson's performance and strengthen their reputation as a true sales hero. The constant practice of these techniques, combined with the continuous search for learning and improvement, is the path to becoming a master of the art of persuasion and negotiation, opening doors to significant opportunities and achievements.

Using empathy as a powerful sales weapon

Empathy is one of the most powerful skills a sales hero can

cultivate on their journey to sales success. More than just a buzzword, empathy is the ability to genuinely understand a customer's feelings, thoughts and perspectives. In this chapter, we'll explore how empathy can be a powerful weapon in the hands of the salesperson, enabling them to build authentic relationships, win the customer's trust and increase their chances of closing successful deals.

True empathy in sales: true empathy goes beyond mere words or superficial actions. It is a skill that comes from the heart and mind of the salesperson, allowing them to put themselves in the customer's shoes in a sincere and authentic way. It is an exercise in active listening and deep understanding of the customer's needs, desires and concerns, without judgment or assumptions.

Creating an authentic connection: when salespeople show genuine empathy, they create an authentic connection with the customer. This connection is the foundation for developing a solid and lasting relationship. The customer feels valued and understood, which makes it more likely that they will open up and share their real needs and interests.

Listening with empathy: empathy in sales begins with the practice of active and focused listening. The sales hero must devote time and attention to the customer, listening to their stories, challenges and aspirations. This practice allows the salesperson to identify opportunities for personalization and offer solutions that meet the customer's specific needs.

Demonstrate understanding and acceptance: once the salesperson has listened carefully to the customer, it is essential to demonstrate understanding and acceptance of their perspectives and feelings. This doesn't necessarily mean agreeing with everything the customer says, but rather validating their emotions and points of view, showing that their concerns are taken seriously.

Adapting the sales approach: empathy allows the salesperson to adapt their sales approach to suit the customer's preferences. Each customer is unique, and the sales hero recognizes that a personalized approach is more effective than a generic pitch. Empathy helps the salesperson identify the customer's communication style and adjust their language to communicate more effectively.

Solving problems with sensitivity: empathy is especially important when dealing with delicate situations or customer objections. Instead of simply dismissing the customer's concerns, the empathetic salesperson seeks to understand the reasons behind the objections and works with the customer to find solutions that meet their needs.

Building trust and loyalty: empathy is the basis for building trust and loyalty. When the customer perceives that the salesperson is genuinely interested in their well-being and success, they become more inclined to trust the salesperson and continue the relationship beyond the initial sale.

Turning customers into brand advocates: customers who experience empathy on the part of the salesperson tend to become brand advocates. They share their positive experiences with others, helping to extend the brand's reach and attract new potential customers.

Dealing with rejection with empathy: the hero salesperson recognizes that empathy is also important when dealing with rejection. Not all negotiations will be successful, and the empathetic salesperson doesn't take rejection personally. Instead, they understand that the customer may have different needs and respect their decision.

A virtuous circle of empathy: empathy creates a virtuous circle of healthy and successful relationships. As salespeople practice empathy with their customers, they inspire other members of the sales team to do the same. This positive cycle fosters a culture of empathy within the company, creating an environment conducive to growth and prosperity.

Empathy is one of the most powerful tools available to the sales hero. It strengthens bonds with customers, increases the likelihood of successful sales and has a positive impact on both financial results and customer satisfaction. Empathy is not just a skill, but a mindset that permeates all the salesperson's interactions. It is a human and authentic approach that respects the customer's individuality and values their experiences and needs.

By putting themselves in the customer's shoes, the sales hero demonstrates that they are committed to finding the best solution for their needs, which builds a reputation of trust and respect. This reputation is valuable because it leads to positive referrals, satisfied customers and long-term relationships.

In order to develop empathy as a powerful sales weapon, salespeople must be willing to strip away prejudices and stereotypes, practice active and genuine listening, seek to get to know their customers deeply and put themselves in their shoes. Empathy is not something that can be simulated; it must be cultivated out of a genuine concern for the customer's well-being and a desire to help them achieve their goals.

With empathy as a guide, the salesperson can become a valuable ally for the customer, offering truly personalized solutions in line with their needs. Empathy also allows the salesperson to anticipate problems and offer proactive support to the customer, becoming a reliable source of guidance and advice.

Empathy is the key to opening the door to the customer's heart. It's what makes the hero salesperson more than just an ordinary salesperson - they become a reliable and compassionate partner, willing to walk alongside the customer towards success. With empathy as an ally, the sales hero can face any sales challenge, creating authentic relationships, closing meaningful deals and leaving a legacy of satisfaction and lasting success.

CHAPTER 7: THE ETHICS OF THE SALES HERO

In this chapter, we will explore one of the fundamental pillars of the sales hero: ethics. Being a successful salesperson is not just about closing deals and achieving targets, but also about acting with integrity, transparency and respect for clients and business relationships. The sales hero understands that their reputation is their most valuable asset and that the basis for sustainable success is rooted in ethical practices.

The sales hero's code of conduct: the sales hero adopts a code of ethical conduct that guides their actions in all interactions with customers, colleagues and business partners. This code includes principles such as honesty, respect, responsibility and transparency. The sales hero understands that ethics are the basis for building trust, credibility and long-term relationships.

Transparency at every stage of the sale: the sales hero doesn't hide important information or use manipulative tactics to gain an advantage. On the contrary, they value transparency at every stage of the sale, from the presentation of the offer to the payment terms. Transparency allows the customer to make informed decisions, creating a relationship of mutual trust.

Respect for the customer's autonomy: the customer is the protagonist of their buying journey, and the sales hero respects their autonomy and decision-making capacity. They don't impose their opinions or try to influence the customer beyond what is necessary. Instead, the sales hero is willing to be a guide and facilitator, helping the customer to make the best decision for their needs.

Avoiding deceptive practices: the sales hero rejects deceptive or dishonest practices that could harm the customer or compromise their own integrity. He doesn't promise what he can't deliver or use false information to manipulate the customer. Instead, the sales hero seeks to build genuine relationships based on truth and trust.

Respect for competition and intellectual property: the sales hero's ethics also extend to relations with competitors and intellectual property. They don't defame or denigrate their competitors, but compete fairly and ethically. In addition, the sales hero respects the intellectual property rights of other companies and does not use confidential or protected information without permission.

Commitment to excellence in customer service: the sales hero is committed to excellence in customer service. This means being available to answer questions, providing after-sales support and ensuring that the customer is satisfied with their purchase. The sales hero understands that service excellence is essential to building a solid reputation and fostering customer loyalty.

The sales hero's social responsibility: the sales hero not only seeks individual success, but also cares about the social and environmental impact of their actions. They engage in responsible practices that consider the well-being of the community and the environment. The sales hero can, for example, promote products or services that are sustainable or contribute to relevant social causes.

Ethical use of data and information: the sales hero respects customer privacy and uses personal data and information responsibly. They protect the confidentiality of customer information and do not use it inappropriately or for unauthorized purposes.

The courage to act ethically: the sales hero's ethics require the courage to make the right choices, even when faced with pressure or temptations to act unethically. The sales hero understands that ethics is an intrinsic value, not just a means to an end.

The satisfaction of being an ethical sales hero: the sales hero finds satisfaction in knowing that his ethical practices contribute to building a solid career, trusting relationships and a reputation for excellence. They understand that being an ethical sales hero is a continuous journey of self-development and improvement, which guides them towards lasting and meaningful success.

Ethics is the compass that directs the sales hero on his sales journey. It is the basis for authentic relationships, customer trust and sustainable success. The sales hero understands that his actions have an impact not only on his own career, but also on society and the environment. He prides himself on acting with integrity, respect and responsibility, and sees ethics as a source of strength and inspiration to face challenges and achieve exceptional results. With ethics as an ally, the sales hero is prepared to face the future with confidence, determination and the commitment to make a positive and ethical difference in the world of sales.

Practicing honesty and transparency to build trust

Honesty and transparency are fundamental pillars of the sales hero ethic. In this chapter, we will explore the importance of these qualities and how they can be used as powerful tools to build and strengthen trust with customers.

The basis of trust: trust is the foundation of any solid relationship, including business relationships. The sales hero understands that in order to win the customer's trust, it is essential to be honest and transparent in every interaction. Honesty creates an atmosphere of sincerity and authenticity, while transparency demonstrates openness and respect for the customer.

The importance of integrity: honesty and transparency are intrinsically linked to the integrity of the sales hero. He understands that his actions must be in line with his values and ethical principles. Integrity is what makes his words trustworthy and his promises kept, generating respect and admiration from the customer.

Honesty in offers and proposals: the sales hero never exaggerates or distorts information to make his offers more attractive. They offer realistic and honest solutions, in line with the customer's needs and expectations. Transparency is a powerful ally in this process, allowing the customer to understand exactly what is being offered and how it meets their demands.

Dealing with limitations and challenges: the sales hero is also transparent about the limitations and challenges of the product or service they are offering. He doesn't try to hide possible problems or shortcomings, but rather presents a realistic view, also highlighting the benefits and advantages that the customer will gain. This honest approach helps the customer make informed decisions and reduces the likelihood of unpleasant surprises in the future.

The impact of transparency on the relationship of trust: practicing transparency has a positive effect on the relationship of trust between the sales hero and the customer. When the customer sees that the salesperson is open and honest at every stage of the sale, they feel safer and more comfortable sharing their concerns and doubts. This open and honest communication strengthens the connection between the parties, facilitating mutual understanding and building a long-term relationship.

The value of honesty in negotiations: honesty is also essential in negotiations with customers. The heroic salesperson doesn't make empty promises or offer conditions they can't meet. They are transparent about limitations and deadlines, always trying to find a balance that is beneficial to both parties. This frank attitude shows respect for the customer and establishes fertile ground for building lasting partnerships.

Generating trust after the sale: honesty and transparency don't end when the sale is closed. The sales hero continues to practice these qualities in after-sales support, fulfilling what was agreed and ensuring customer satisfaction with the purchase. The trust generated during the sale extends to the ongoing relationship with the customer, encouraging loyalty and positive referrals to others.

Ethics as a competitive differentiator: in the competitive world of sales, the ethics of the sales hero become a powerful differentiator. Customers value honesty and transparency, and are more likely to choose suppliers who demonstrate these qualities. In addition, the ethical reputation of the sales hero attracts potential customers and strengthens the company's brand.

The sales hero's responsibility: the sales hero understands that acting ethically is not just a choice, but a responsibility. They recognize the impact of their actions on customers, the company and society as a whole. This awareness motivates them to act with integrity, even when faced with pressures or temptations to act less ethically.

An ongoing commitment: practicing honesty and transparency is an ongoing commitment for the sales hero. They know that ethics is not a one-time goal, but a journey of self-development and constant improvement. The sales hero is always looking to improve, learning from his experiences and striving to be the best possible professional.

Honesty and transparency are essential qualities of the sales hero. They build trust, strengthen relationships and generate sustainable results in the world of sales. The sales hero understands that, although the temptation to adopt less ethical practices may arise, it is the choice of integrity that makes them a true sales hero. The continuous practice of honesty and transparency is a journey of self-discovery and growth, which guides you to lasting and significant success in your career as a salesperson.

Cultivating long-term relationships with customers

The sales hero understands that sales is not just about closing momentary deals, but also about building lasting relationships with customers. In this chapter, we'll explore the importance of cultivating these bonds and how the sales hero can turn customers into loyal partners over time.

The vision beyond the short term: while some salespeople focus only on achieving immediate goals, the sales hero adopts a long-term perspective. They understand that true success in sales lies in building solid, sustainable relationships that generate benefits for the customer and the company over time.

Listening as a powerful tool: the sales hero understands that active listening is the basis for understanding the customer's needs and desires. They not only listen to what is being said, but also seek to understand what is not being said. This in-depth listening skill allows the sales hero to offer truly personalized solutions, strengthening the connection with the customer.

The importance of follow-up: the sales hero doesn't end the relationship with the customer once the sale has been made. On the contrary, they follow up continuously, ensuring that the customer is satisfied with the purchase and offering support whenever necessary. Following up shows the customer that they are valued and that the sales hero is committed to helping them succeed with their purchase.

The practice of consistent communication: the sales hero understands that communication is essential to maintaining healthy relationships. They maintain consistent and relevant communication with the customer, whether through calls, emails or face-to-face meetings. This communication is not restricted to commercial offers, but also includes useful information, tips and content that can add value to the customer.

Empathy as a connection tool: empathy is a powerful skill that the sales hero uses to truly connect with the customer. They seek to understand the customer's experiences, challenges and goals, and act as a partner who is genuinely interested in their success. This emotional connection strengthens ties with the customer and creates a relationship of mutual trust.

Offering continuous solutions: the sales hero doesn't see the sale as the end of the relationship, but as the beginning of a lasting partnership. They continually seek to offer solutions that meet the customer's evolving needs. This may involve product or service updates, new offers aligned with the customer's objectives or even suggestions for improvements to their business process.

Solving problems with agility: no relationship is without its problems. The sales hero sees challenges as opportunities to demonstrate his dedication to the customer. They approach problems with agility, seeking quick and efficient solutions. The way the sales hero deals with adversity can be a decisive factor in strengthening the relationship and consolidating the customer's trust.

Celebrating achievements together: the sales hero celebrates the customer's achievements as if they were their own. They share the customer's joy at moments of success and recognition. This joint celebration strengthens the feeling of partnership and reinforces the emotional bond between the sales hero and the customer.

The importance of flexibility: each customer is unique, with individual needs and preferences. The sales hero understands the importance of being flexible and adapting to each customer's style and pace. They are willing to customize their approach and offer to suit the particularities of each situation.

The satisfaction of long-term relationships: the sales hero finds satisfaction and fulfillment in cultivating long-term relationships with customers. These lasting partnerships not only generate positive financial results, but also provide the feeling of fulfilling a mission: helping customers achieve their goals and overcome challenges.

The sales hero's ability to cultivate long-term relationships with customers is essential for long-term success in the world of sales. The practice of honesty, empathy, active listening and consistent communication is what allows the sales hero to establish genuine connections with customers, building a solid foundation of trust and loyalty. These lasting partnerships not only drive business growth, but also bring meaning and satisfaction to the sales hero, who finds fulfillment in building valuable, lasting relationships with those they serve.

CHAPTER 8: OVERCOMING AND SELF-OVERCOMING

The sales hero faces constant challenges on his journey through the world of sales. In this chapter, we will explore the importance of overcoming and self-overcoming for the success of the sales hero. We'll understand how they deal with adversity, seek continuous improvement and turn obstacles into opportunities for growth.

The hero's mindset: the sales hero adopts a resilient mindset when faced with challenges. They understand that, as with any heroic journey, they will face obstacles and setbacks. However, his positive attitude and determination propel him forward, even in the face of difficulties.

Turning challenges into opportunities: while some salespeople may get discouraged by rejections or missed targets, the heroic salesperson sees these situations as opportunities to learn and grow. He analyzes the challenges, identifies the lessons that can be learned and seeks to improve his strategies for the future.

Learning from failures: the sales hero is not afraid of failure, as he understands that it is part of the growth process. They see failures as valuable learning opportunities. Each defeat is a chance to analyze his mistakes, improve his skills and become stronger for the next business battles.

Setting challenging goals: for the sales hero, overcoming is not just about achieving set goals, but also about setting challenging objectives. He constantly seeks to raise the level of his aspirations and strives to reach ever higher heights in his career. This incessant quest to surpass their own limits is what drives their professional growth.

The importance of self-development: the sales hero is constantly seeking self-development. They recognize that in order to overcome obstacles and stand out in the market, it is essential to improve their skills, knowledge and competencies. Investing in training, reading and qualifications is a recurring practice for the sales hero.

Cultivating emotional resilience: emotional resilience is one of the main characteristics of the sales hero. They understand that the field of sales can be challenging, with emotional ups and downs. That's why they develop skills to deal with stress, pressure and uncertainty, remaining firm and balanced even in the most difficult situations.

Seeking support and collaboration: the sales hero doesn't face adversity alone. They seek support and collaboration within the sales team, sharing experiences, ideas and strategies. The exchange of knowledge and mutual collaboration strengthen not only the sales hero, but the whole team, which becomes more resilient and capable of overcoming challenges collectively.

Adopting persistence: persistence is an indispensable virtue of the sales hero. They don't flinch in the face of "no" and don't give up easily. The sales hero understands that sales is a continuous journey and that each new contact is a new opportunity to win a customer. Their persistence drives them forward, even when there seem to be insurmountable obstacles.

Celebrating victories: just as the sales hero faces challenges, he also celebrates victories with enthusiasm and gratitude. With every deal closed, goal achieved and customer satisfied, he celebrates the fruit of his effort and dedication. This celebration not only strengthens his motivation, but also keeps the pleasure of working in the world of sales alive.

Overcoming as a way of life: for the sales hero, overcoming is not just a goal to be achieved, but a way of life. He understands that the road to success is a continuous journey of learning, growth and improvement. Overcoming is what drives the sales hero to embrace each new challenge, confident in his ability to become better and better at his profession.

Overcoming and self-overcoming are fundamental for the sales hero to achieve success in sales. They face challenges with resilience, learn from failures, set challenging goals and constantly seek to improve their skills. The sales hero sees every obstacle as an opportunity for growth, making him not only a more competent professional, but also a more resilient, motivated and inspiring human being for those around him. His incessant quest to overcome is what makes him a true sales hero.

Learning from their mistakes and striving for constant evolution

The sales hero understands that, as in any growth journey, mistakes are valuable opportunities for learning and development. In this chapter, we will explore the importance of recognizing and learning from one's mistakes, as well as the continuous search for evolution as a sales professional.

Constructive self-criticism: the sales hero has the courage to look at himself honestly and self-critically. They understand that nobody is perfect and that they make mistakes, but they see these situations as opportunities to grow. Constructive self-criticism allows the sales hero to identify points for improvement in their sales approaches and seek solutions to improve their performance.

Turning mistakes into learning opportunities: the sales hero understands that mistakes are not definitive failures, but learning opportunities. They analyze each situation in which something didn't go as expected and try to understand what could have been done differently. This deep reflection allows the sales hero to extract valuable lessons and apply them in his future interactions with customers.

Adopting a growth mindset: a growth mindset is a fundamental pillar for the sales hero. They believe that their skills and competencies can be improved over time through effort and dedication. This mindset drives them to face challenges and constantly seek to evolve as a sales professional.

Seeking external feedback: the sales hero is not afraid to

seek external feedback, whether from colleagues, managers or clients. They understand that receiving different perspectives is valuable for identifying blind spots and opportunities for growth. Feedback is a powerful tool that the sales hero uses to improve their skills and offer even more efficient customer service.

Valuing experimentation: the sales hero is not afraid to try out new approaches and strategies. They understand that experimentation is a way of discovering what works best for them and their customers. Even if some attempts don't have the expected result, the sales hero values the experience gained and believes that each attempt brings him closer to sales excellence.

Learning as a continuous process: for the sales hero, learning is a continuous process that has no end. He constantly seeks out courses, training and materials that can broaden his knowledge and improve his sales skills. The sales hero understands that constant evolution is what keeps them competitive and relevant in the market.

Persistence in the search for evolution: the sales hero is not content with the status quo. He persists in the quest for evolution, even when the challenges seem difficult to overcome. The sales hero's determination drives him to keep learning and developing, even in the face of seemingly insurmountable obstacles.

Sharing knowledge with the team: the sales hero doesn't keep his learning experiences to himself. They share their lessons and knowledge with the team, creating an environment of collaboration and mutual growth. The exchange of learning between team members strengthens the group as a whole and allows everyone to evolve together.

Learning from success: the sales hero understands that success is also a source of learning. He analyzes his best achievements, trying to understand which strategies and approaches were responsible for these positive results. Learning from success is just as important as learning from mistakes, as it enables the sales hero to replicate their best practices in other situations.

The journey as a reward: for the sales hero, the constant search for evolution is rewarding in itself. Every new skill acquired, every lesson learned from mistakes, every step towards sales excellence is a valuable reward. The journey of self-improvement is what motivates the sales hero to remain passionate about their profession and to aim for a successful and fulfilling future.

Learning from their mistakes and constantly striving to evolve are central characteristics of the sales hero. They don't allow themselves to be overwhelmed by challenges, but see them as opportunities for growth. The continuous search for self-development, combined with the humility to recognize that there is always something new to learn, is what allows the sales hero to become increasingly competent, efficient and inspiring in their sales journey. Self-improvement is what keeps him always striving for excellence, allowing him not only to achieve success in sales, but also to enjoy the personal and professional fulfillment that only constant evolution can provide.

Managing the stress and pressure of everyday sales life

Everyday life in sales is dynamic and challenging, full of targets, deadlines and expectations to meet. In this chapter, we'll discuss the importance of managing stress and pressure for the sales hero, and how they can maintain emotional balance and exceptional performance even in the most intense moments.

Recognizing the signs of stress: the sales hero understands that stress is a natural response of the body to the demands of everyday life. They learn to recognize the signs of stress, such as muscle tension, irritability, difficulty sleeping and lack of concentration. By identifying these signs early, the sales hero can adopt management strategies before stress becomes detrimental to their performance.

Practicing self-care: the sales hero recognizes the importance of self-care in dealing with stress and pressure. He makes time for activities that give him pleasure and relaxation, such as physical exercise, meditation, reading or hobbies. Self-care is essential for recharging energy and keeping the mind and body healthy, enabling the sales hero to face the challenges of everyday life with more emotional balance.

Setting limits: the sales hero understands that setting limits is fundamental to avoiding work overload and the consequent increase in stress. He sets times to dedicate to professional activities and times for rest and leisure. By setting clear boundaries, the sales hero avoids physical and mental exhaustion, guaranteeing their productivity and efficiency in the long term.

Focusing on time management: the sales hero knows that time is a valuable and scarce resource. They seek to improve their time management skills to avoid the feeling of always racing against the clock. The sales hero sets priorities, organizes his tasks and avoids procrastination, optimizing his time and reducing the stress related to not having enough time to meet his obligations.

Finding support in the team: the sales hero seeks support in the team when feeling overwhelmed or facing stressful situations. Collaboration with colleagues and managers allows the sales hero to share responsibilities, receive help in difficult times and feel supported in a mutually supportive environment.

Emotional resilience: emotional resilience is a key competency for the sales hero to cope with stress and daily pressure. They understand that they won't always have control over external situations, but they can control their emotional response to them. The sales hero develops the skills to deal with adversity in a healthy way, finding solutions and standing firm in the face of challenges.

Seeking moments of rest: the sales hero understands that moments of rest are essential to recharge their batteries and increase their productivity. They value breaks during the working day to relax and get away from the demands of the business. These moments of rest allow the sales hero to resume their activities with more focus and disposition.

Maintaining a positive outlook: the sales hero practices positive thinking even in the face of challenges and pressures. They understand that the perspective from which they view situations can influence their emotional response. By maintaining an optimistic outlook, the sales hero becomes more resilient and able to find creative solutions to problems.

Developing relaxation strategies: the sales hero adopts relaxation strategies to release accumulated stress. They can resort to physical exercise, deep breathing, relaxation techniques or even talking to colleagues about their worries. These strategies allow the sales hero to find emotional relief and maintain balance during times of pressure.

Learning from stressful experiences: the sales hero understands that stressful experiences are valuable learning opportunities. He reflects on how he handled these situations, identifies what worked and what could be improved. From these reflections, the sales hero develops skills to manage stress in an increasingly effective and positive way.

The sales hero understands the importance of managing the stress and pressure of everyday sales. They recognize the signs of stress, practice self-care, set limits, seek support from the team, develop emotional resilience and adopt relaxation strategies. The sales hero understands that stress management is fundamental to exceptional performance and to maintaining emotional balance on their journey through the world of sales.

CHAPTER 9:
INSPIRING A TEAM
OF SALES HEROES

Just as the sales hero is able to conquer the market with his courage and exceptional skills, inspiring a team of sales heroes is key to achieving extraordinary results. In this chapter, we will explore strategies and practices for sales leaders who want to boost their team's potential by motivating them to act like true sales heroes.

Setting an inspiring vision: the sales leader must set an inspiring vision for the team, presenting a clear picture of the desired future. The vision must be challenging and aligned with the organization's values and objectives, motivating each team member to push themselves beyond their limits in pursuit of this greater purpose.

Cultivating a culture of sales heroes: a company culture that celebrates and values the heroic spirit of salespeople is essential for inspiring the team. The leader must foster a culture of recognition, where salespeople's efforts and achievements are publicly celebrated, encouraging them to assume a heroic identity in their daily activities.

Identifying and developing talent: the sales leader must get to know the team individually, identifying each salesperson's strengths and areas for improvement. Investing in the development of sales skills is crucial to empowering team members to reach their full potential, making them true heroes in their specialties.

Setting challenging and realistic goals: challenging but achievable goals encourage the team to overcome their own limits and pursue sales heroism. The leader must involve the salespeople in setting the targets, ensuring that they are committed and motivated to achieve them.

Communicating with inspiration: the sales leader must master the art of inspiring communication. It is essential to convey the team's vision, goals and values with enthusiasm and clarity, stimulating the salespeople's passion for their work and a sense of purpose in their actions.

Fostering collaboration and camaraderie: team spirit is key to inspiring a team of sales heroes. The leader must encourage collaboration, knowledge sharing and cooperation between team members, creating an environment of mutual support and companionship.

Empowering salespeople to make decisions: giving salespeople the autonomy to make decisions is a way of empowering them and encouraging them to take a leading role in their activities. The leader must trust in the team's ability and encourage them to make informed decisions, providing a sense of responsibility and commitment.

Recognizing and celebrating achievements: recognition is a powerful motivational tool. The sales leader must publicly recognize the team's individual and collective achievements, providing a sense of appreciation and reward for heroic efforts towards commercial results.

Promoting professional development: the sales leader must invest in the continuous development of the team, offering training, workshops and learning opportunities. A constantly evolving salesperson is more confident, resilient and willing to face challenges like a true hero.

Leading with empathy and integrity: empathy and integrity are essential values for inspiring a team of sales heroes. The leader must be an example of ethical conduct and understanding, always there to support the salespeople on their professional and personal journeys.

Inspiring a team of sales heroes requires visionary leadership, cultivating a culture of heroes, recognizing and continuously developing talent, inspiring communication and empathy. The sales leader who adopts these practices empowers the team, encouraging them to act with courage, determination and excellence in their commercial activities. By transforming the team into a group of sales heroes, the leader boosts productivity and results, reaching new heights of success and conquering the market with a united team motivated to overcome any challenge.

Leading by example and motivating the team to success

Leadership is a fundamental skill for inspiring and motivating a team of salespeople towards success. In this chapter, we will explore the importance of leading by example, demonstrating courage, resilience and integrity, and how this positively impacts team performance. In addition, we'll discuss strategies for motivating salespeople, encouraging them to act like true sales heroes.

The power of example in leadership: an inspiring leader is one who practices what he preaches. Leading by example means being aligned with the company's values, showing integrity, honesty and commitment in all actions. A leader who lives the principles he or she teaches earns the respect and trust of the team, becoming a role model.

Cultivating team trust: trust is the foundation of a solid and motivated team. The leader must show confidence in each salesperson's ability, delegating responsibilities and allowing them to take on challenges. By showing confidence, the leader encourages the salespeople's professional growth, allowing them to develop their skills and become sales heroes.

Creating a supportive environment: the leader must create a supportive and encouraging environment where salespeople feel safe to express their ideas, ask questions and share their concerns. A positive environment strengthens the feeling of belonging to the team and encourages collaboration.

Recognizing and valuing achievements: recognition is a powerful tool for motivating the team. The leader must recognize and value individual and collective achievements, praising the effort and performance of salespeople. Public recognition strengthens salespeople's self-esteem, encouraging them to constantly strive for excellence in their activities.

Setting challenging targets: the leader must set challenging but realistic targets for the team. Ambitious targets encourage salespeople to step out of their comfort zones, seek new challenges and achieve exceptional results. The leader must support and guide the team on their journey to achieve these goals, making themselves available to help them with their needs.

Promoting professional development: a leader who is committed to the development of their team invests in training, workshops and learning opportunities. The leader should encourage salespeople to constantly seek to improve their skills, becoming increasingly prepared to face the challenges of sales.

Sharing success stories: success stories are sources of inspiration for the team. The leader can share stories of salespeople who have overcome obstacles, won over important clients or achieved surprising results. These stories motivate the team and show that success is achievable with effort and dedication.

Encouraging autonomy and creativity: the leader must encourage the autonomy and creativity of salespeople, allowing them to make decisions and find innovative solutions to everyday challenges. The freedom to act and the search for creative solutions empowers salespeople, making them more engaged and confident in their activities.

Being a mentor and coach: a truly inspiring leader is also a mentor and coach to the team. The leader must be available to guide, give constructive feedback and support salespeople in their professional development. The leader's role as a mentor is fundamental to the team's individual and collective growth.

Celebrating teamwork: finally, the leader must value teamwork and celebrate collective achievements. Recognizing the importance of collaboration and mutual support motivates salespeople to join forces towards common goals.

Leading by example and motivating the team to succeed is a combination of attitudes and practices that strengthen the corporate culture and the performance of the sales team. The inspiring leader is the one who leads by example, cultivating the team's trust, recognizing and valuing achievements, setting challenging goals, promoting professional development and encouraging autonomy and creativity. With an inspiring leader at the helm, the team becomes more engaged, motivated and committed to acting like true sales heroes, achieving extraordinary results and consistently succeeding.

Creating a culture of sales excellence

A culture of sales excellence is the foundation for boosting team performance and consistently achieving exceptional results. In this chapter, we will explore the importance of creating a company culture focused on the pursuit of excellence at every stage of the sales process. From hiring new salespeople to celebrating achievements, a culture of excellence permeates all the team's actions, inspiring them to act like true sales heroes.

Defining the vision and values of a culture of excellence: the first step in creating a culture of excellence is to define the vision and values that will guide the sales team's actions. The vision must be ambitious and inspiring, showing the level of excellence that the team seeks to achieve. The values must reflect the ethical and behavioral principles that will guide the salespeople's decisions and attitudes.

Hiring the right heroes: a culture of excellence starts with hiring. The sales leader must seek out talent that is aligned with the team's vision and values, looking for salespeople who are committed, resilient and determined to achieve excellence in their activities.

Setting challenging targets: Challenging targets push the team to leave their comfort zone and constantly strive to excel. The leader must set ambitious but realistic goals that motivate salespeople to give their best in the pursuit of success.

Promoting continuous learning: a culture of excellence values continuous learning. The leader should encourage participation in training, workshops and events that add knowledge and skills to salespeople. Investing in professional development strengthens the team and prepares them to face ever greater challenges.

Encouraging collaboration and the exchange of knowledge: teamwork is essential for a culture of excellence. The leader must encourage collaboration between salespeople, promoting the exchange of knowledge and experiences. Collaboration strengthens the team, allowing each member to contribute their unique skills.

Valuing feedback and continuous improvement: a culture of excellence embraces feedback as a valuable tool for continuous improvement. The leader should encourage the practice of constructive feedback, encouraging salespeople to reflect on their performance and identify opportunities for improvement.

Recognizing and celebrating achievements: recognition is a key element in strengthening a culture of excellence. The leader must value individual and collective achievements, celebrating the efforts and results made. Public recognition encourages salespeople to persist in their pursuit of excellence.

Stimulating creativity and innovation: a culture of excellence encourages creativity and the search for innovative solutions. The leader must encourage salespeople to think creatively, looking for differentiated approaches and innovative strategies to win customers and overcome challenges.

Keeping the focus on customer satisfaction: sales excellence is directly linked to customer satisfaction. The leader must encourage the team to focus on the customer, understanding their needs and offering solutions that exceed their expectations. A culture focused on customer satisfaction reinforces the team's commitment to excellence in all interactions.

Remaining flexible and adaptable: a culture of excellence is not static; it must be flexible and adaptable to changes in the market and customer needs. The leader must encourage the team to adapt quickly to changes in the sales landscape, looking for opportunities and acting quickly to stand out from the competition.

Seeing challenges as opportunities for growth: in a culture of excellence, challenges are seen as opportunities for growth. The leader must help salespeople face obstacles with determination, learning from adversity and seeking solutions to improve their results even further.

Cultivating pride in belonging to the team: a culture of excellence makes salespeople proud to be part of the team. The leader must create a positive and welcoming environment where salespeople feel valued and motivated to contribute to the team's success. A sense of belonging strengthens team engagement and reinforces commitment to excellence.

Creating a culture of excellence in sales is an ongoing process that involves defining an inspiring vision, hiring the right talent, setting challenging goals, encouraging continuous learning and collaboration, valuing feedback and recognition, stimulating creativity and innovation, keeping the focus on customer satisfaction and being adaptable to market changes. A culture of excellence empowers staff, inspiring them to act like true sales heroes, achieving extraordinary results and consistently succeeding. By cultivating a culture of excellence, the leader creates an environment conducive to the professional and personal growth of salespeople, building a team that is united and highly motivated to face any challenge with determination, passion and excellence.

CHAPTER 10: THE SALES HERO OF THE FUTURE

The sales landscape is constantly evolving, driven by technological advances, changes in consumer preferences and new market trends. In this chapter, we will explore the profile of the "sales hero of the future", who adapts to the changes of the modern world and uses the tools available to stand out as a true sales champion. Through innovative skills, mindset and strategies, the sales hero of the future becomes an agent of change and success in an increasingly competitive market.

Growth mindset: the sales hero of the future adopts a growth mindset, always seeking to learn and develop. They are open to new ideas, technologies and trends, constantly seeking to improve their skills and knowledge in order to remain relevant in a dynamic environment.

Emotional intelligence as a differentiator: in an increasingly connected world, emotional intelligence becomes a competitive differentiator for the Sales Hero of the Future. They understand the importance of developing empathy, understanding the emotions of customers and teammates, and using this skill to create genuine and lasting connections.

Mastery of emerging technologies: the Sales Hero of the Future understands that technology is a powerful ally in their sales. They master automation tools, data analysis, artificial intelligence and other emerging technologies to improve their efficiency and accuracy in identifying opportunities and meeting customer needs.

Personalization as a strategy: in an increasingly personalized market, the sales hero of the future knows that the "one size fits all" approach is no longer enough. They use data and information to understand the individual preferences and needs of each customer, creating personalized and impactful experiences.

Sustainability and social responsibility: the sales hero of the future understands the importance of sustainability and social responsibility in business. They seek partnerships with companies aligned with ethical and environmental values, and use sustainable practices to win the trust of customers and build a solid reputation.

Collaboration and networking: the sales hero of the future knows that teamwork and collaboration are fundamental to success. They seek out strategic partnerships, exchange knowledge and share best practices with colleagues from other areas, creating a network of support and synergy to achieve even more impactful results.

Adaptability and resilience: in a volatile and uncertain world, adaptability and resilience are essential for the sales hero of the future. They face change with courage and flexibility, learning from adversity and finding opportunities in the midst of challenges.

Entrepreneurship and innovation: the sales hero of the future is an entrepreneur, able to identify business opportunities and innovate in their approaches. They are willing to experiment with new strategies and take calculated risks in order to achieve success.

Focus on the customer experience: the sales hero of the future understands that the customer experience is the key to loyalty and positive word of mouth. They constantly seek to exceed customer expectations by offering personalized, agile and delightful service.

Long-term vision: the sales hero of the future has a long-term vision, seeking to build lasting and sustainable relationships with customers. They understand that customer loyalty is earned over time through consistent and genuine service.

The sales hero of the future is an adaptable, innovative and customer-oriented professional. They use emerging technologies, emotional intelligence and personalized strategies to stand out in an increasingly competitive market. In addition, they understand the importance of social responsibility, collaboration and sustainability in business. With their growth mindset, focus on the customer experience and long-term vision, the sales hero of the future becomes a successful protagonist in the world of sales, inspiring and positively impacting everyone around them.

Glimpsing the infinite potential for professional and personal growth

In the world of sales, as in life, the potential for growth is unlimited. In this chapter, we'll delve into the journey of the sales hero in search of full development, both professionally and personally. By glimpsing the infinite potential that dwells within each salesperson, we will uncover powerful strategies and mindsets that drive them to reach ever higher heights, transforming them into true protagonists of their lives and careers.

Believing in inner potential: the starting point for glimpsing infinite potential is believing in inner power. The sales hero recognizes that he has unique talents and abilities, and understands that growth begins with believing in oneself. They learn to silence negative voices, overcome self-criticism and cultivate solid self-confidence, nurturing a mindset of success.

Setting audacious goals: the sales hero understands that growth is a continuous and exciting journey. They set audacious and challenging goals that encourage them to go beyond their limits and explore their full potential. Each goal achieved is celebrated as a step towards personal and professional growth.

Persistence and resilience: on the road to infinite growth, the sales hero encounters obstacles and challenges. Persistence and resilience are his allies on this journey. They learn to turn adversity into learning opportunities, standing firm in the face of difficulties and finding the strength to keep moving forward.

Constantly seeking knowledge: knowledge is a powerful fuel for growth. The sales hero constantly seeks new learning, whether through books, courses, mentoring or practical experiences. They understand that learning is a gateway to expanding their potential.

Embracing change and innovation: infinite potential is intrinsically linked to the ability to embrace change and innovation. The sales hero remains open to new ideas, trends and technologies, understanding that adaptation is essential for continuous growth.

Learning from failure: failure is a valuable learning opportunity on the road to growth. The sales hero doesn't fear failure; he sees it as a stepping stone to success. He learns from his mistakes, corrects course and uses these experiences to become stronger and more resilient.

Cultivating meaningful relationships: professional and personal growth is driven by meaningful relationships. The sales hero values connections with colleagues, mentors, clients and family members. These relationships strengthen him by providing support, guidance and inspiration on his growth journey.

Managing time wisely: infinite potential can only be realized with wise time management. The sales hero prioritizes his activities, establishing a productive routine that allows him to invest in his professional and personal development.

Challenging the comfort zone: growth is beyond the limits of the comfort zone. The sales hero is willing to face discomfort and try out new situations. They understand that growth happens outside the comfort zone.

Cultivating gratitude: gratitude is a powerful force that drives the sales hero's growth. He recognizes and is grateful for the opportunities, achievements and lessons learned in his life and career. Gratitude amplifies their positivity and motivation to achieve even more.

By glimpsing the infinite potential for professional and personal growth, the sales hero transcends the limitations imposed by the past and spreads his wings to fly towards a future of unexplored possibilities. He understands that the journey of growth is continuous, and that each step taken is a significant achievement in his incessant quest for excellence. Each victory, each learning experience and each evolution are bricks that build the path to the pinnacle of his potential, transforming him into an inspiring protagonist of his own story.

Embracing the continuous journey of self-discovery and improvement

In the world of sales, the journey to success is marked by an incessant quest for self-discovery and improvement. In this chapter, we will explore the importance of embracing this continuous journey, delving deep inside ourselves to understand our motivations, values and passions. By getting to know ourselves better, we uncover our strengths and areas for development, boosting our professional and personal growth. The journey of self-discovery and improvement is an invitation to unlock our deepest potentials and become the heroes of our own story.

Self-knowledge (the basis of growth): the journey of self-discovery begins with self-knowledge. The sales hero seeks to look inside himself with honesty and authenticity, recognizing his virtues, talents, fears and limitations. Understanding who we are and how we relate to the world is the basis for building a meaningful growth journey.

Awakening awareness of self and others: by embracing the continuous journey of self-discovery, the sales hero also develops awareness of others. They seek to understand the needs, desires and perspectives of customers, colleagues and others involved in their career. This ability to empathize strengthens their interpersonal connections and has a positive impact on their sales.

Accepting the learning process: the sales hero understands that growth is a continuous learning process. They embrace challenges as learning opportunities and see mistakes as stepping stones. With each experience, they seek to learn and improve, maintaining a humble attitude towards knowledge.

Flexibility and adaptation: on the journey of self-discovery, the sales hero cultivates flexibility and the ability to adapt. They recognize that change is inevitable and are willing to adjust their strategies and approaches as necessary. Flexibility allows them to flow with market changes and grow with them.

Defining values and purpose: to be a true protagonist of his journey, the sales hero defines his values and purpose. They understand that clearly defining their guiding principles will guide them through difficult decisions, and that having a well-established purpose will keep them motivated and committed to their goals.

Learning from self-reflection: self-reflection is a powerful ally in the journey of self-discovery. The sales hero takes the time to observe and analyze his actions, behaviors and results. This practice allows them to identify points for improvement and celebrate their achievements, pushing them to achieve even more exceptional performance.

Leaving the comfort zone: to fully exploit the potential for growth, the sales hero must be willing to leave the comfort zone. They embrace the unknown and face their fears, knowing that it is outside the comfort zone that true growth and innovation occur.

Developing resilience: the journey of self-discovery is not always easy. The sales hero develops the resilience to deal with the adversities and challenges that come his way. They find the strength to overcome difficulties, learn from them and move forward with determination.

Seeking balance: in the quest for self-discovery and improvement, the sales hero also understands the importance of balancing personal and professional life. He strives to reconcile his responsibilities and find time to take care of himself and his interpersonal relationships.

Celebrating the journey: the journey of self-discovery and improvement is one of constant growth and transformation. The sales hero celebrates each step taken towards personal and professional development. He recognizes that, every day, he becomes a more complete human being capable of achieving his goals.

By embracing the continuous journey of self-discovery and improvement, the sales hero embarks on a path of deep and meaningful growth. He becomes aware of his infinite potential, develops essential skills and uses his self-knowledge to create genuine connections with clients and colleagues. The journey is transformative, revealing the true hero in each of us. In this chapter, we encourage the sales hero to commit to this ongoing journey, allowing themselves to uncover the deepest layers of themselves and becoming the protagonist of a story of success, growth and achievement.

CHAPTER 11:
PRACTICAL TOOLS OF
THE SALES HERO

In this appendix, we've put together a set of practical tools so that the sales hero can enhance his skills and boost his performance even more in the world of sales. These tools are designed to be applied on a daily basis, helping you to achieve exceptional results and stand out as a true protagonist in your negotiations. From persuasion techniques to time management strategies, each tool is designed to enable the sales hero to face challenges and achieve success in a consistent and inspiring way.

Personalized approach script: a well-crafted approach script is one of the sales hero's most powerful tools. It creates a personalized guide for starting conversations with potential customers, ensuring that each interaction is relevant, engaging and effective. The script should be adaptable, allowing the sales hero to adjust according to the client's profile and the nature of the negotiation.

Active listening techniques: active listening is a fundamental skill for the sales hero. It involves listening to the customer with full attention, understanding their needs, desires and concerns. By using active listening techniques, the sales hero shows empathy, gains the customer's trust and identifies opportunities to offer customized solutions.

Objection and response matrix: the sales hero anticipates common objections that may arise during the sales process and creates a matrix of assertive and persuasive responses. This tool allows you to be prepared to circumvent objections and provide convincing arguments to persuade the customer to make favorable decisions.

Customer follow-up plan: a structured follow-up plan is essential for maintaining a lasting relationship with customers. The sales hero creates a schedule of contacts and interactions, ensuring that no customer is overlooked and that they are always there to meet their needs.

Self-development calendar: for the sales hero, self-development is a constant priority. He creates a calendar to regularly dedicate time to learning, whether it's reading books, attending courses or training. This schedule is essential for constantly improving their skills and knowledge.

After-sales strategies: the relationship with the customer doesn't end after the sale. The sales hero develops after-sales strategies to foster ongoing engagement and customer feedback. These strategies include collecting testimonials and reviews, as well as offering ongoing support to ensure customer satisfaction.

Time management plan: efficient time management is an indispensable tool for the sales hero. It creates a detailed plan to prioritize tasks, set daily goals and ensure that every minute is used productively. The time management plan allows him to focus on activities that generate significant results in his sales.

Strategic networking: the sales hero understands the value of networking and builds a strategic network of contacts. He attends industry events, partners with other professionals and gets involved in relevant discussion groups. Strategic networking expands his business opportunities and keeps him connected to the market.

Performance indicators: to track his progress and results, the sales hero uses specific performance indicators. These indicators include sales targets, conversion rate, average ticket and other relevant KPIs. By monitoring these indicators, he can identify areas for improvement and celebrate his achievements.

Growth mindset: the growth mindset is the basis for applying all the sales hero tools. They cultivate a positive and resilient mindset, seeing challenges as opportunities to learn and grow. This mindset drives their motivation, determination and ability to achieve exceptional results.

By using these practical tools of the sales hero, the professional becomes a sales master, able to face the challenges of the market with confidence and excellence. Each tool is a valuable resource for honing your skills, developing genuine relationships and standing out as a true sales leader. The sales hero understands that, with the right tools in hand, he is prepared to achieve success consistently, becoming an agent of change and inspiration in his professional journey. Apply these tools with dedication and commitment and become a true sales hero, ready to face any challenge and achieve extraordinary results.

Checklist for a powerful sales pitch

A powerful sales pitch is the sales hero's secret weapon for gaining attention, arousing interest and closing deals persuasively. In this chapter, we present a comprehensive checklist for the sales hero to create and improve their sales pitch, ensuring that it is engaging, persuasive and effective. Each element of the checklist is designed to help the sales hero convey their message clearly, connecting deeply with customers and inspiring them to take action.

Know your audience: before creating a sales pitch, the sales hero must get to know their target audience in depth. Research and understand the needs, desires, pains and aspirations of potential customers. The more personalized the speech, the greater the connection with the audience.

Define the objective: the sales pitch must have a clear and specific objective. The sales hero must decide what action they want the customer to take after hearing the speech, whether it's closing a sale, scheduling a meeting or giving a demonstration.

Start with a powerful hook: grab the audience's attention right from the start with a powerful hook. It could be an intriguing question, an impactful statistic or an engaging story that arouses interest and holds the listener's attention.

Tell a story: stories have the power to move, inspire and connect. The sales hero can incorporate relevant and engaging stories into their pitch to illustrate the value of the product or service on offer and create an emotional connection with the customer.

Highlight the benefits: emphasize the benefits of the product or service, focusing on the positive results the customer will get from purchasing it. The sales hero must highlight how their product or service will solve problems and meet the customer's needs.

Present social proof: social proof, such as testimonials from satisfied customers, positive reviews and success stories, is powerful for building the customer's trust in what is being offered. Use this evidence to back up the claims you make in your speech.

Use persuasive language: choose persuasive words and phrases that arouse interest and encourage the customer to act. Use terms like "exclusive", "immediate benefit", "satisfaction guarantee" to create a sense of urgency and importance.

Show empathy: show empathy when addressing the customer's concerns and objections. The sales hero must listen carefully and respond with understanding, ensuring that the customer feels valued and respected.

Offer customized solutions: personalize the pitch to meet the specific needs of each customer. Show that the sales hero understands individual demands and is ready to offer tailor-made solutions.

Make a call to action: end the speech with a clear and convincing call to action. The sales hero should guide the customer on the next step to take, whether it's filling in a form, scheduling a demonstration or making a purchase.

Practice, practice, practice: practice is essential to improve the sales pitch. The sales hero should practice their speech several times, whether alone, to teammates or in front of a mirror, until it flows naturally and conveys confidence.

Ask for feedback: seek feedback on your sales pitch from

teammates or mentors. They can offer valuable insights and help identify areas for improvement.

Adapt to feedback: be open to suggestions and constructive feedback. The sales hero must be willing to make adjustments to the speech to make it more impactful and persuasive.

Stay authentic: the sales pitch must reflect the personality and values of the sales hero. It is important to be authentic and genuine when presenting the product or service to customers.

By following this checklist, the sales hero will be ready to create a powerful and effective sales pitch, capable of winning the customer's trust, overcoming objections and driving success in negotiations. Remember that constant practice and the continuous search for excellence are fundamental to improving the speech over time. With dedication, empathy and a personalized approach, the sales hero inspires clients and achieves extraordinary results on their journey through the world of sales.

Exercises to strengthen the heroic mindset

The heroic mindset is the basis for the success and continuous growth of the Sales Hero. In this chapter, we will present a series of powerful exercises that have been designed to strengthen the heroic mindset, boosting the sales professional's confidence, resilience and determination. These exercises can be incorporated into the sales hero's daily routine, allowing them to face challenges with courage and achieve exceptional results.

Gratitude diary: create the habit of keeping a gratitude diary, in which the Sales Hero writes down at least three things they are grateful for every day. This simple practice helps cultivate a positive mindset, focusing on what is working and what is valued.

Goal visualization: take a few minutes every day to visualize your sales goals being achieved. Imagine yourself closing deals, meeting customer needs and exceeding targets. Visualization helps strengthen your belief in your own ability to succeed.

Positive affirmations: create positive and powerful affirmations related to sales performance. Repeat these affirmations daily, for example: "I am a sales hero, capable of winning big deals and lasting relationships."

Challenge yourself regularly: to strengthen the heroic mindset, it's essential to face challenges that take the sales hero beyond their comfort zone. Set ambitious goals and go for them, even if it means taking calculated risks.

Reframe failures: instead of seeing failures as defeats, see them as opportunities to learn and grow. Analyze the lessons that can be drawn from each experience and apply this knowledge to improve future approaches.

Find a mentor: Look for an experienced mentor or colleague who can offer guidance and support on your journey. Exchanging ideas with someone who has been through similar challenges can be invaluable for personal and professional growth.

Read inspirational books: reading inspirational and motivational books can nurture the heroic mindset. Look for books by authors who share stories of overcoming and success in the world of sales.

Do meditation and breathing exercises: practice meditation and breathing exercises to calm the mind, reduce stress and increase mental clarity. This helps the sales hero stay focused on the present and make conscious decisions.

Learn from adversity: instead of feeling defeated in the face of challenges, try to learn from adversity. Analyze what worked and what didn't, identifying opportunities for improvement.

Stay connected: share your experiences with other salespeople and take part in discussion groups or online forums. Exchanging ideas and connecting with professional colleagues is valuable for enriching the hero mentality.

Celebrate your achievements: when you achieve goals and sales success, celebrate your achievements. Recognize your efforts and reward yourself for every victory, no matter how small.

Practice self-compassion: allow yourself to make mistakes and recognize that nobody is perfect. Practice self-compassion and be kind to yourself in times of difficulty.

Develop resilience: strengthen your resilience when facing setbacks. See them as learning opportunities and use them as a springboard for growth.

Evaluate regularly: periodically review your goals and progress. Make an honest assessment of your performance and identify areas for improvement.

By incorporating these exercises into the routine, the heroic salesperson strengthens himself emotionally and psychologically, preparing himself to face challenges and achieve success in sales. The heroic mindset is an inexhaustible source of inspiration and motivation to overcome obstacles and achieve ever more audacious goals. By embracing this mindset, the heroic salesperson is on the path to continuous personal and professional growth, becoming a true leader in the world of sales and inspiring others to follow suit.

REGINALDO OSNILDO

I'm Reginaldo Osnildo, your communication strategy expert and mentor on the journey to digital success.

With a career rooted in academy, as a professor and researcher at the University of Southern Santa Catarina, and a practical career as a strategist at Grupo Catarinense de Rádios, I've developed a unique set of skills. My doctorate specializing in sales narratives and digital convergence, together with my master's degree focused on storytelling and social imagery, allows me to create strategies that transform businesses.

What do I offer?

- Personalized communication strategies that resonate with your target audience.

- Advanced storytelling techniques to strengthen your brand.

- Up-to-date insights into digital trends to keep your company ahead of the curve.

Now, imagine your company establishing an authentic and powerful presence in the market, achieving results you never thought possible. I'm here to make it happen.

Your time to act is now! The digital world doesn't wait. Every day is a new chance to move forward, to stand out. Are you ready to take your company to the top? Don't let this opportunity slip away.

Get in touch and let's pave the way to digital success together. I'm just a phone call or email away.

Sincerely

Reginaldo Osnildo, PhD.

+55 48 991913865

reginaldoosnildo@gmail.com

www.ingramcontent.com/pod-product-compliance
Lightning Source LLC
Chambersburg PA
CBHW070433290526
45791CB00005B/1951